THE DEAD SEA PEOPLE'S SACRED MEAL AND JESUS' LAST SUPPER

Leonard F. Badia

University Press of America

Copyright © 1979 by

University Press of America, Inc.™

4710 Auth Place, S.E., Washington, D.C. 20023

All rights reserved

Printed in the United States of America

ISBN: 0-8191-0807-3
Library of Congress No.: 79-66231

Dedicated to My Three brilliant Professors and friends, Dr. Elsie Hug, Dr. Norma Thompson, Dr. Cyrus Gordon of New York University

CONTENTS

PREFACE iv

INTRODUCTION v

I   THE HISTORICAL BACKGROUND OF QUMRAN 1

        Identification 1
        Geographic Location 2
        Time of Location 3
        Reason for Occupation 3

II   THE QUMRAN SACRED MEAL 4

        Archaeological Evidence 8
        Comparison of Brownlee's and Vermes'
          translations of the Manual of Discipline
          and the Messianic Rule Fragment 9
        Biblical Scholars Opinions 14
        Summary 17

III   JESUS' LAST SUPPER 19

        The Synoptic Gospel Accounts 19
        Interpretation of Terms Bread and Wine 24
        Biblical Scholars Opinions 26
        Jesus' Possible Contact with Qumran 30
        Summary 32

IV   COMPARISONS AND CONCLUSIONS 34

        Comparisons 34
        Conclusions 39

APPENDIX 41

FOOTNOTES 47

BIBLIOGRAPHY 62

PREFACE

The purpose of this work is to present an examination and critical evaluation of the Qumranian Sacred Meal and Jesus' Last Supper. Since the discovery of the Dead Sea Scrolls in 1947, some scholars have suggested that Jesus may have been influenced by the Qumranians (the Dead Sea People). Furthermore, this influence showed itself in his Last Supper.

I have attempted to explore this area of contention with a new approach. It is hoped that this work, which is part of my Doctorial dissertation for New York University, will add more light to a very complex problem.

Chapter I contains the historical background of the Qumran community: their identification, geographic location, time of occupation and the reason for their occupation.

Chapter II explores the Qumranian Sacred Meal which is mentioned in their Manual of Discipline Scroll and the Messianic Rule Fragment. In this section, four areas are considered: 1) the archaeological evidence of animal bones 2) a comparison of two noted biblical scholars, Willian Brownlee and Geza Vermes, translations of the Manual of Discipline Scroll and the Messianic Rule Fragment 3) various biblical scholars opinions about the Qumranian Sacred Meal 4) a summary.

Chapter III examines Jesus' Last Supper, which is mentioned in the Synoptic Gospels. Five areas are considered:
1) the synoptic gospel accounts of Jesus' Last Supper
2) interpretation of the Bread and Wine used by Jesus
3) Biblical scholars opinions about Jesus' Last Supper
4) Jesus' possible contact with Qumran 5) a summary.

Chapter IV summarizes the comparisons between the Qumran Sacred Meal and Jesus' Last Supper. It also gives some conclusions which we can draw from these comparisons.

INTRODUCTION

One of the greatest archaeological discoveries of this century happened by accident. It was the spring of 1947. It was the area which is called Qumran, sixteen miles east of Jerusalem in present day Israel. Several young shepherds of the Taamireh tribe of the Bedouin, nomadic arabs, were watching their sheep and goats when suddenly one of the goats strayed off up a steep rocky slope towards the cliffs that formed the north west edge of the Dead Sea Valley. One of the boys, Mohammad, chased the goat who ran into one of the caves. Suddenly, he threw several stones into the cave in order to frighten the animal. At first there was nothing but the sounds of the stones hitting the rocky surface of the cave. Then it happened. Mohammad heard the unmistakable sound of breaking pottery. Frightened by this sound, he returned to his friends. The next day Mohammad came back to the cave with one of his friends and they removed the lid from one of the jars. They emptied out the contents and went to Bethlehem. There they bargained with a shopkeeper named Khalil Iskander Shahin, known locally as Kando. Mohammad and his friends sold their unknown treasure to Kando. What was this treasure? The Dead Sea Scrolls as they were to be known to the world.

The Dead Sea Scrolls, discovered by an Arab Bedouin in 1947, created a revolutionary impact on biblical scholarship throughout the Western World. For the people of Israel, they have made audible the voices of long dead kinsmen, other Jews who lived and worked in the land of Israel centuries ago. For the people of the Christian world, they have revealed the spiritual home of Jesus.

CHAPTER I

THE HISTORICAL BACKGROUND OF QUMRAN

The Qumran community was composed of Jews who considered themselves as the elect remnant of Israel, who would emerge in the last days from the purging judgment of God. In order to prepare for this judgment, they advocated a renewal of the covenant of Moses by a strict repentance and a new obedience to the requirements of the covenant. Naturally, this greatly influenced their lives.

Identification of the Qumran Sect

There is no certainty as to what the members of the Qumran sect called themselves. The term, Qumran, has been ascribed to them by contemporary scholars. However, some scholars referred to them as Zealots, Pharisees, Sadducees and Essenes. Among the authorities concerned with this problem are Cecil Roth[1] and Geoffrey Driver,[2] who believe they were Zealots. The Zealots, who were opposed by some Pharisees according to Finkelstein,[3] rejected all compromise with Rome and acknowledged only God as the ruler of Palestine. Russell says of the Zealots, "It is wrong to regard them simply as a radical group within the state who stirred up trouble with the Romans... they were essentially a company of Jewish patriots motivated by deep religious convictions."[4] On the other hand, Bright thinks the Zealots were "fanatically brave and reckless men who were ready to strike for independence regardless of the odds."[5] However, Pryke[6] and other scholars do not share Roth's and Driver's hypothesis because it does not support the literary, archaeological, and palaeographical evidence found at Qumran.

Burrows[7] agrees with some scholars that it is highly improbable Qumran was a Pharisaic community. Yet, Davies[8] believes some Pharisees may have been in Qumran but it is most unlikely that they comprised a very large segment of the population.

Finally, could the people at Qumran be Essenes? And, if so, were the Essenes, as described in the writings of Josephus, Philo, and Pliny the Elder, the same people who settled at Qumran (4 B.C. - 68 A.D.). Most scholars accept the theory that the Qumranians were a branch of the Essene movement.

Although many scholars have presented considerable evidence in support of the Essene theory, it is not a proved fact. Yet it is the soundest theory. In order to avoid confusion, refer to the people of Qumran as Qumranians.

Geographic Location of Qumran

The site of Qumran may be the ancient salt city, the valley of Anchor, the site of Secacah, or none of these.[9] Khirbet Qumran is the name of the site that lies approximately four to ten miles south of Jericho in Palestine.[10] The etymology of the word Qumran is obscure. It is called Khirbet by the Arabs meaning a hill with ruins on it or for ruins alone.[11] The area of Qumran has been called the Wilderness.[12]

The meaning of wilderness is questioned. The Hebrew word "midbar" means pasture, wildness, steppe,[13] or frequently a defined tract of wilderness or the wilderness of a particular region.[14] The Hebrew word "midbar" also means grazing land and the Greek word "Eremos" means a lonely, uncultivated, uninhabited place.[15]

Burrows expresses skepticism about the meaning of wilderness; others claim it was nothing more than a non-local expression in Near East mythologies. Yet, geological and meterological data seem to justify its meaning as the wilderness of Sinai or the wilderness of Judea.[16] In any case, the wilderness was a natural place for those who were dissatisfied with existing conditions as well as for those who wished a rendezvous place relatively free of detection. Whether it is accepted in the wider or the narrower sense of the word, the wilderness of Judea is the activity area of the Qumran people.[17]

Time of Occupation

Archaeology shows there were three main periods of occupation of the Qumran site, as follows: the first quarter of the first century, B.C., or earlier to 31 B.C. when a severe earthquake shook Judea; 4 B.C. to June 68 A.D. when the Roman army under Vespasian destroyed it; 132-135 A.D. during the short-lived second Jewish revolt.[18] However, it is the second occupation of the area of Qumran (4 B.C. - 68 A.D.) which concerns us.

Reason for Occupation

The conditions of Palestine in the first century A.D. were not stable. According to Roth,[19] the Romans were not in complete military control of the country but were a great menace to the Palestinian Jew. Both politically and religiously, the Jewish priests were the authorities during the first century A.D. when the Judaean area of Palestine was in perpetual fever of religious excitement. Finkelstein[20] says it was inevitable that there would be a clash between Rome and Palestine. Rome avoided internal interference as much as possible; however, the Roman procurators of Judaea were mostly irresponsible men. Whether some Jews went to Qumran from different areas of Palestine for political, military, or strictly religious motives, or a combination of these motives is not certain, but it seems to have been primarily for religious motives.[21]

CHAPTER II

THE QUMRAN SACRED MEAL

The people of Qumran were Jews. Their beliefs in general were those of other Jews and were based on the Hebrew Bible and particularly on the Law or the Torah, that is, the five books of Moses. God is the source of the Torah from which man can draw the secret wisdom and knowledge of the essence of things. If they were faithful to the prescriptions of the Torah, they would receive salvation. Therefore, they demanded good conduct and strict legal observance of the Torah from every full-fledged member and every novice.

The Qumran doctrine of God is basically that of the Hebrew Bible. God, who will reward the good and punish the bad, is the creator and sovereign ruler of the universe.

The Qumran doctrine concerning man is also fundamentally that of the Hebrew Bible. The sect believed that although man was made in the image and the likeness of God, nevertheless he was weak, impure, and sinful; but, he could be saved by the faithful observance of the Torah, which was demanded.

The Qumran doctrine of Eschatology is fairly clear. In the narrower sense,[22] eschatology is the doctrine of the end of the world, while in the wider sense[23] it means the world to come or the future. It is commonly expressed in terms such as "on that day," "at the end of the days," "this age," and "the age to come."[24] In addition, there were expressions such as "this world," "the days of the Messiah," and "the world to come," and others.[25] According to Moore,[26] there was an indefiniteness and indistinctiveness in these eschatological terms for the Jews after the third century, A.D. However, the Qumranians believed that they were the last generation in the last days and that they awaited the final judgment as immediately imminent.[27] What the "last days" meant to the Qumranians is not clear, since there is on one comprehensive meaning of these eschatological terms such as "last days," "end of days," "coming world," and "future."[28] What is certain is that they believed they were living in those days and therefore had an eschatological hope. This eschatological hope was centered around the appearance of the Messiah or Messiahs and the prophet.[29] At the present time, it is impossible to determine whether they expected one or two Messiahs.[30] In either case when he or they appeared, the final blessing of the righteous would take place.[31] Again, it is impossible to ascertain whether this blessing would be earthly and materialistic or heavenly and spiritualistic.[32]

It is also difficult to determine whether the Qumran eschatology was Messianic or Apocalyptic. Apocalypticism began roughly between 200 B.C. and 100 A.D.,[33] and it proposed that the Son of Man or Heavenly Redeemer would appear and usher in a new age.[34] These apocalyptists believed they had been commissioned by God to reveal the secrets of the Scriptures to their fellow men, and they stressed the spirit of the observance of the Torah rather than the legal precepts of the Torah.[35] Messianism, which can be traced beyond the tenth century, B.C., of Judaism, taught that the Jewish people would be saved not by any cultural or political institutions but through the intervention of God.[36] How and when God would intervene is not certain, but what is certain is that he would intervene some day.[37]

Scholars, such as LaSor and Burrows, believe that the Qumran eschatology was Messianic rather than Apocalyptic.[38] The Qumran concepts of Messianism are not well-defined and developed.[39]

The term Messiah, meaning anointed, was often applied to kings, prophets and priests. It is not certain how the Qumranians interpreted the term and if they expected one or two Messiahs.[40]

The theory of one Messiah is held by Sutcliffe[41] and LaSor,[42] but scholars like Brownlee,[43] Pfeiffer,[44] Kuhn,[45] Milik,[46] and Burrows[47] favor the theory of two Messiahs. However, Ringgren[48] is not sure whether the Qumranians were expecting one Messiah or two. In brief, the one-Messiah theory meant that the Messiah would be a lay person from the lineage of King David, who had united and reigned over Israel as well as Judah.[49] LaSor[50] believes that the one-Messiah theory means that the Qumranians expected one Messiah who would be called the Davidic Messiah or the Messiah of Israel, and he would be a lay person representing all the people of Israel.

Those scholars who hold the two-Messiah theory believe that the Qumranians awaited two Messiahs, the Messiah of Aaron who would be a priest from the priestly lineage of Aaron and the Messiah of Israel who would be a layman from the lineage of King David.

In the time of the Second Temple, there was the idea of two messianic figures, the high priest and the Messianic king.[51] All Messianic concepts depended upon the spiritual and theological approach of the various Jewish trends, but the Messiah or Messiahs were always human beings even if sometimes supernatural qualities were ascribed to them.[52] Scholars who favor the two-Messiah theory state that, strictly speaking, only the Messiah of Israel is the true Messiah in the real sense of the term; he is the nasi, the prince, the lay head of the eschatological community.[53] Since the high priest was also anointed, the latter could also be called a Messiah.

As has been stated, many scholars support the two-Messiah theory. Although the evidence that identifies the Messiahs is inconclusive, the same thing can be said about the third figure of the Qumran Messianic eschatology, namely, the prophet. The expectation of a prophet who would come in the last days is based on Deuteronomy 18:18, "I will raise up for them a prophet like you from among their brethren; and I will put my words in his mouth, and he shall speak to them all that I commanded him." Scholars have attempted to identify the Prophet with the figure to whom they refer as the Teacher of Righteousness. For example, Sutcliffe[54] says the Teacher of Righteousness was not the original founder of the Qumran sect but was a member of the community who influenced and guided the members in the path of God's law. Allegro[55] suggests that he was probably a high priest of Israel who lived between 104 and 78 B.C. The Teacher of Righteousness was simply a great teacher of the Qumran community who instructed the people in the interpretation of the Scriptures.[56] Brownlee[57] claims that this teacher was a priest of the first century, B.C., who was probably crucified. In opposition to this idea, Cecil Roth[58] thinks the Teacher was Menehem or Eleazor ben Jair, who was a religious leader (66 A.D. - 73 A.D.) of the Zealot movement. Burrows[59] Vermes,[60] and Cross[61] believe the Teacher of Righteousness to be a priest.

Thus, the evidence to identify the Teacher of Righteousness as the Prophet is inconclusive and perhaps the best explanation is given by Helmer Ringgren: "The Teacher of Righteousness was not understood as a Messiah but rather as a prophetic forerunner to the two Annointed One........ Doubtless he is a figure who was considered to have inaugurated or at least prepared for the new, messianic era."[62]

This prophet-type of Messiah is peculiar to the rabbinic apocalyptic literature, and He is called the Messiah, son of Joseph or son of Ephraim.[63] According to this literature, he will precede the Messiah, son of David and will die in battle with the enemies of God and Israel.[64] When and how this concept of Messiah, son of Joseph, originated is a question that has not been answered satisfactorily.[65]

These religious ideas of the Qumranians is expressed in their Sacred Meal Rite.

Perhaps of all the aspects of Qumran studies none has aroused more controversy than the meaning and significance of the Sacred Meal of the Qumran Community. The passages under investigation are found in the Manual of Discipline (6:2-6) and the Messianic Rule Fragment (2:11-22).

The Manual of Discipline is one of the eleven scrolls discovered in the Qumran caves by the Bedouin Arabs of Palestine in 1947.[66] Although the data of its original composition is disputed, Burrows says that the Manual was written between 175 B.C. and 40 B.C.[67] The title, Manual of Discipline, was given to the scroll by Millar Burrows because of the original title, if there was one, was damaged or lost before it came into his possession.[68] Other titles, such as the Rule of the Community[69] and the Rule of the Covenant,[70] have also been given to this scroll. The Manual of Discipline contains the beliefs and practices of the Qumran community; detailed rules that governed life, organization and discipline also were found in it. There are references to the ritual washings and the common meals, which is the prime focus of this study.

The sacred meal of the Qumranians is mentioned in the Manual of Discipline (6:2-6) and the Messianic Rule Fragment (2:11-22). Vermes[71] states that the Messianic Rule Fragment was originally a part of the Manual of Discipline scroll.

Schubert[72] says that it may be. Sutcliffe[73] maintains that the Messianic Rule Fragment was composed at a different time than the Manual of Discipline. Scholars, therefore are not in agreement on whether these documents were originally one document or two distinct documents composed at different times. In any case, the Messianic Rule Fragment describes a meal which is similar to that found in a passage in the Manual of Discipline (6:2-6). However, the former adds a procedure that is not found in the Manual of Discipline. The Messianic Rule Fragment (2:11-22) says, if the Messiah (Messiahs) is present at the meal, he will take his place next to the chiefs of the community and he will give a blessing over the bread and wine after the priest has given his blessing over them.

Now let us consider the Qumranian Sacred Meal under four areas: Archaeological evidence of animal bones; a comparison of Brownlee's and Vermes' translations of the Sacred Meal section of the Manual of Discipline and Vermes' translation of the Messianic Rule Fragment; biblical scholars' opinions about these Sacred Meals and finally a summary.

Archaeological Evidence

Speculation about the type of meals celebrated at Qumran was heightened by the discovery of bones deposited between large shards of pitchers or pots, or sometimes placed in covered jars. The bones came from sheep, goats, and lambs and were certainly the remnants of meals.[74] According to Schubert,[75] these were consecrated bones of blessed animals eaten at the Qumranian meals. Harrison[76] says that these bones show there were special meals. In line with Harrison's idea, Allegro[77] maintains that these bones could not have come from ordinary meals, because there would have been thousands of bones. Cross[78] claims that these bones are the remains of sacred feasts. There are scholars who are cautious in their interpretations. For example, Sutcliffe[79] says "Nothing is known of the significance of certain curious deposits of animal bones (goats, sheep, oxen) found at Qumran." More explicit in his caution is Van Der Ploeg[80] who says, "The mere fact that bones of animals which were eaten as food have been found in the vicinity of the buildings of Hirbet Qumran does not tell anything of their origin, sacred or profane.

Neither Brownlee's nor Vermes' translations (MD 6:2-6), (VMR 2:11-22) mentions any animals that might have been eaten at these meals. Since the translations are silent on this point, the cautious statements of such scholars as Sutcliffe and Van Der Ploeg seem unwarranted.

COMPARISON OF BROWNLEE'S AND VERMES' TRANSLATIONS OF THE MANUAL OF DISCIPLINE AND THE MESSIANIC RULE FRAGMENT

Aside from the minor differences in Brownlee's and Vermes' translations of the <u>Manual of Discipline</u> and Vermes' translations of the <u>Messianic Rule Fragment</u>, there are agreements on certain points. The two translations indicate: 1) There was an observance of rank at the meals. 2) The Qumranians apparently ate in units of ten with a priest among them. 3) The priest blessed the bread and/or wine. 4) It is not clear whether food other than bread and wine was eaten at these meals. 5) Bread and wine are specifically mentioned in this passage. 6) It is not clear whether the <u>Manual of Discipline</u> (6:2-6) refers to the daily common meals, special meals, sacred meals, or any other type of meals. 7) It is not certain whether the <u>Messianic Rule Fragment</u> (2:11-22) refers to an actual meal at which the Messiah will be present or a "heavenly" banquet that will take place.

For clarity, I have divided the <u>Manual of Discipline</u> (6:2-8) according to various points of interest.

1. The Rule of Obedience

The two translators speak of the rule of obedience. The younger person must obey the older member with regard to work and possessions. Apparently, seniority is an important feature of community life.

Brownlee	Vermes
The Lesser shall obey the greater in regards to goods and means.	The man of lesser rank shall obey the greater in matters of work and money. (6:2)

2. Communal Living

According to both translations, the members of the Qumran community were mindful of doing everything in common. For example, they ate, prayed and took counsel in common.

Brownlee

They shall eat communally, and bless communally, and take counsel communally. (6:3)

Vermes

They shall eat in common, and pray in common, and deliberate in common. (6:3)

3. A Male Community

Neither translation says anything about women eating at the meals. It can only be presumed that women did eat at the meals. It is simply stated that they will eat in groups of ten men among whom there will be a priest. It has been suggested that the Qumran community was predominently a male community, but it is a debatable point.

Brownlee

And in every place where there are ten men of the council of the Community, there shall not cease from among them a man who is priest. (6:3-4)

Vermes

Wherever there are ten men of the Council of the community there shall not lack a Priest among them.

4. Observance of Rank

Apparently, there was strict observance of rank in seating at meals. Both translations are in agreement on this point.

Brownlee

And let each one according to his assigned position or rank sit before him. (6:4)

Vermes

And they shall all sit before him according to their rank. (6:4)

5. Table

Brownlee's and Vermes' translations indicate that they ate at tables. It must be presumed that they did not recline on couches, which was an ancient custom.

Brownlee	Vermes
And it shall be when they arrange the table to eat. (6:4-5)	And when the table has been prepared for eating. (6:4-5)

6. Bread and Wine

Each translator indicates that bread and wine were on the table at meals. However, Vermes calls the wine a new wine. Although there may have been other food at these meals, these two translators mention only bread and wine.

Brownlee	Vermes
The priest shall first stretch out his hand to invoke a blessing with the first of the bread and the wine. (6:5-6)	The Priest shall be the first to stretch out his hand to bless the first fruits of the bread and new wine. (6:5-6)

7. Priest

From the Qumran literature, it is apparent that the priest had an important function in the community. Brownlee's and Vermes' translations (MD: 6:4, 5-6) indicate that he gave the blessing over the bread and wine. It might be called grace before meals.

Brownlee	Vermes
The priest shall first stretch out his hand to invoke a blessing with the first of the bread and the wine. (6:5-6).	The Priest shall be the first to stretch out his hand to bless the first fruits of the bread and new wine. (6:5-6)

The comparison of Brownlee's and Vermes' translations of the <u>Manual of Discipline</u> (6:2-6) shows the great similarity between the two translations. There are only slight variances here and there. For example, Brownlee (MD 6:5-6) says wine while Vermes (MD 6:5-6) says new wine. However, on all significant points they are in agreement with each other.

It is impossible to make a comparison of the <u>Messianic Rule Fragment</u> (2:11-22), because Brownlee has not translated this part of the Dead Sea Scrolls. However, an analysis of Vermes' translation (MR 2:11-22) is important to the sacred meal problem.

For purposes of clarity, I have divided and analyzed the <u>Messianic Rule Fragment</u> (2:11-22) according to categories.

1. <u>Messiahs</u>

It is clear that Vermes is speaking of two Messiahs in these verses. In his culmentary, he identifies them as the King-Messiah who was to be the Prince of the Congregation, and the Priestly Annointed, the Messiah of Aaron and Israel.[81]

> He shall come at the head of the whole congregation of Israel with all his brethren the sons of Aaron the Priests, those called to the assembly, the men of renown; and they shall sit before him, each man in order of his dignity. And then the Messiah of Israel shall come, and the chiefs of the clans of Israel shall sit before him, each in the order of his dignity, according to his place in their camps and marches.

2. <u>People at Dinner</u>

According to Vermes' translation, men of renown, chiefs of the clans, heads of family, and wise men gather together for the meals. Because of their strictness on purity, this passage probably refers to all the full-fledged members of the community.

> Those called to the assembly, the men of
> renown...the chiefs of the clans of
> Israel...and before them shall sit all
> the heads of family of the congregation,
> and the wise men of the holy congregation.

3. Bread and Wine

Vermes' translation indicates that bread and wine were on the table at these meals. There is no mention of any other food.

> Let no man extend his hand over the
> first fruits of bread and wine before
> the Priest.

4. Priest

In his translation, Vermes says that it is the priest who blesses the bread and wine at the meal. In reading his commentary on the passage, it is clear that Vermes means the Priest-Messiah.

> Let no man extend his hand over the
> first fruits of bread and wine before
> the Priest; for it is he who shall
> bless the first-fruits of the bread
> and wine, and shall be the first to
> extend his hand over the bread.

5. The Messiah of Israel

Vermes says that the Messiah of Israel who is the King-Messiah[82] will give his blessing over the bread after the Priest-Messiah has done it. Once again, the importance of the priesthood is demonstrated.

6. Men

Vermes' translation points out that this procedure will be followed at each meal at which at least ten men are present. It says nothing about women.

Therefore, it can be concluded from Vermes'[83] translation of the <u>Messianic Rule Fragment</u> (2:11-22) that it is a description of a meal to be attended by the Priest-Messiah and the King-Messiah. According to Vermes, the meal described in the <u>Messianic Rule Fragment</u> may be alluding to the Messianic Banquet that will take place one day. Some scholars do not share Vermes' interpretation. Because of Vermes' scholarly reputation, his translation and interpretation cannot be easily dismissed.

BIBLICAL SCHOLARS' OPINIONS

In ancient religions, meals in which the participants ate and drank together for purposes of creating religious bonds with one another such as the covenant or fostering a union between God and human participants, are commonly called sacred meals.

1. Qumran Meals Were Sacred Meals

A number of scholars believe that the meals at Qumran were sacred. For instance, Pfeiffer,[84] Smyth,[85] and LaSor[86] simply say that the meals referred to in the two passages were sacred meals. Because their meals were blessed, Dupont-Sommer[87] suggests that they were sacred. Similarly, Ringgren[88] claims that they were sacred because the priest assumed the place of the head of the household. An interesting point is made by Groh,[89] who says that they had sacred meals such as a modified Passover meal at the time of the covenant renewal. Since there were no guests and anyone doing penance was excluded from these meals, Vermes[90] maintains that they were sacred meals. On the other hand, Milik[91] says that normally there were no sacred meals and that the <u>Messianic Rule Fragment</u> refers to a sacred banquet that will be held in the last days.

Allegro[92] agrees with Milik. However, Pryke,[93] and Brown, Fitzmyer, and Murphy[94] are of the opinion that the two passages refer to their regular meals, which were considered sacred because of the character of the community and were an anticipation of the great day when the two Messiahs would appear. It is not clear what most of these scholars mean by the word sacred. In Brownlee's and Vermes' translations

(MD 6:2-6), (VMR 2:11-22) the word sacred is not used in their description of the meals at Qumran.

2. Qumran Meals Were the Daily Common Meals

Other scholars hold the opinion that the meals mentioned in these two passages were the daily common meals of the community. Driver,[95] Rowley,[96] Yadin,[97] and Mann[98] claim that these meals were the ordinary daily meals with procedures to be followed in the event of the coming of the Messiah.

Similarly, Van Der Ploeg[99] claims that they were daily meals with neither sacred nor Messianic meaning. Sutcliffe[100] also refers to these meals as daily meals with no sacramental or symbolic significance. As for Schubert,[101] he feels that the reference is to two meals, one the regular daily meal and the other a special meal, when only full-fledged members could participate. Finally, Burrows[102] sums up this view by saying that these were the daily common meals and had nothing to do with the Messiah, who, when he comes, will have his part in the proceedings.

3. Qumran Meals Were a Liturgical Anticipation of the Messianic Banquet

Some scholars like McKenzie,[103] Cross,[104] Kilmartin,[105] and Vermes[106] believe that the Qumranians had a sacred meal that was a liturgical anticipation of the Messianic Banquet to come. Whether or not these scholars thought this Messianic Banquet could be on earth or in heaven is not clear. However, Davies[107] says that the Qumranian meals were eaten in anticipation of the Messiah or Messiahs' appearance, because he or they probably had not yet arrived. Wilson[108] expresses the view that this special meal has not yet taken place but would take place when the Messiah came and then these meals would continue in the era after his coming. Priest[109] seems to be implying that these meals would take place here on earth rather than in heaven. Bruce[110] claims that there are two types of meals being spoken of in these passages. One is the regular daily meal and the other is the sacred meal in anticipation of the Messiah's coming.

There seems to be vagueness at times as to whether scholars mean these meals will be eaten in heaven or on earth. Also, some scholars may have taken liberty in reading into the translations of the texts something that was not there. Vermes' translation (MR 2:11-22) gives no indication as to whether the meal would be eaten in heaven or on earth.

4. Qumran Meals Were Special Religious Meals

Again, there are some scholars who interpret the Messianic Rule Fragment to mean that sometimes there were special religious meals in addition to the daily common meals at Qumran. It is the opinion of De Vaux[111] that this is exactly what is meant in the Messianic Rule Fragment. Muller[112] describes it as "the yearly feast of the renewal of the covenant." Perhaps, these special meals were the regular evening meal of the Sabbath or a particular feast day.[113]

Although Jewish apocryphals and Rabbinic writings fostered a strict interpretation of the Sabbath, festive banquets were considered proper on this day. However, food was prepared on the preceding day so as not to violate the Law which forbade all cooking on the Sabbath. Special food on the Sabbath was observed, because in the Deuteronomic Decalogue the reason for Sabbath observance is the Exodus. Apparently, festivals were observed by special food preparations and appropriate forms of blessing and thanksgiving.

5. Qumran Meals Were Sacramental Meals

There are only a few scholars who think that these meals were sacramental. Authorities like Huhn[114], and Fritsch[115] are proponents of this theory. However, Pfeiffer[116] says that these meals were perhaps sacramental. Harrison[117] goes into great detail in his explanation, saying that there were special meals of a sacramental character and eventually the Messiah would appear at one of these meals. It is not clear what these scholars mean by sacramental. Since all four of the scholars who think of these meals as sacramental are Christian scholars, it is possible that they are interpreting these passages in light of Christian terminology. In the broad sense of the word, Sacramental means the rite and ceremony that accompanies the observance of divine worship and the administration of the Sacraments.[118] In the narrow sense, Sacramental means a certain rite, action, or particular thing that the church uses in imitation of the Sacraments, in order to obtain through the church's intercession certain spiritual effects.[119]

6. Qumran Meals Were Either Eschatological or Special Meals

There are some scholars who would rather wait for further translations of unpublished material from Qumran than make too hasty an interpretation. For example, Raymond Brown[120] simply says that, at this time, he would say these meals referred to in the Messianic Rule Fragment mean eschatological meals. Black[121] makes the observation that the Manual of Discipline passage refers to a special meal for the members of the highest rank and the council members of the community. In the Messianic Rule Fragment he observes that there is a reference to a special meal to come, at which the priestly hierarchy and the ranking order of the sect will be observed.

SUMMARY

The Qumranians were Jews who voluntarily separated from their contemporaries in Palestine to live an austere and ascetic life. Among their religious practices were common meals that some scholars call sacred meals, religious meals, eschatological meals, or messianic banquets. Unfortunately, the literature from Qumran is of little help in identifying what their meals were. Furthermore, in the case of the meals at Qumran, archaeologists have discovered animal bones but apparently the purpose for which they were used cannot be identified specifically. From the passages, translated texts and the writings of many scholars, it is impossible to say whether or not the meal or meals described in the two passages of their literature were sacred, religious, eschatological, messianic, special, or just common meals. These descriptions by scholars are not found in the translated texts themselves. Therefore, it seems that it is still too early to make assumptions about the type of meals these were, since about half of the Qumran literature has not yet been translated. One must move with extreme caution and be constantly aware of the possibility of prejudicing people when using the words, "sacred," "religious," "eschatological," and "Messianic." These words usually have different meanings to different people. Unless the scholar clearly defines the term he is using, I believe he should not use it. Christian scholars, in particular, must be extremely cautious in their interpretations, because they naturally are influenced by their beliefs, especially the belief that the Old Testament was a preparation for the New Testament. For example, for some scholars the sacred meal might be a pre-figure of the Last Supper of Jesus.

At this point, I believe that it is too soon to settle the above problems. When the remainder of the Qumran literature is translated, when perhaps a clearer picture of the language of the sect and of the religious practices at Qumran will emerge.

Finally, the data suggest that the members of the Qumran community had a strong conviction that they were living in the last days. Therefore, they prepared for the final days by a strict observance of the Torah (the Law).

It is not clear from their literature whether they believed in one or two Messiahs. It is also my opinion that the Qumranians had daily communal meals that might be considered sacred, since the participants ate and drank together for the purpose of strict observance of the covenant. The priest who was an important member of the community blessed the food at their meals. The priest's blessing added to the sacredness of a meal, since he fulfilled the command by God to Moses in the book of Numbers 6:27, "They shall invoke My Name on behalf of the Israelites and I will bless them." The biblical command on which the obligation of grace at meals is founded occurs in the book of Deuteronomy 8:10, "And you shall eat and be full, and you shall bless the Lord your God for the good land he has given you." It seems reasonable to assume that on special religious feasts, these meals were a little more elaborate in food and prayers. There would be appropriate blessings for the different festivals which the priest would recite on those occasions. Finally, I believe that the Qumranians were deeply religious Jews who were searching for a better way to live in accordance with their religious beliefs.

CHAPTER III

JESUS' LAST SUPPER

We have examined the Qumranian Sacred Meal. Now, let us look at the Last Supper of Jesus as is recorded in the Synoptic Gospels.

For clarity, let us consider Jesus' Last Supper under five areas: the synoptic accounts of the Last Supper; the Bread and Wine used by Jesus; Biblical scholars opinions; Jesus' possible contact with Qumran, and finally a summary.

THE SYNOPTIC GOSPELS

The Last Supper of Jesus is recorded in the Synoptic Gospels (Matthew 26: 17-29; Mark 14:12-25; Luke 22:7-20). The first thing one notices when comparing the three accounts, after their common traits, are the similarities that exist between Matthew and Mark. The substantial agreement among the accounts indicates that they may have been derived from one source. In any case, it seems evident that Matthew, Mark and Luke's gospels are of the primitive church. Second, the synoptic writers seem to have "liturgized" the oral traditions of Jesus' Last Supper. Third, all the accounts of his Last Supper lack historical details, which one might expect of a writer who is narrating an important event. In all the accounts, the writers seem to be describing Jesus' Last Supper as a Passover meal or at least a festive meal with a Passover coloring. In all the accounts, the unessential details of the meal are placed in the background. The synoptic writers seem to have kept only the remembrance of the essential actions of Jesus which would be required in the future to carry out the re-presentation of the Last Supper.

1. Time of the Last Supper

The time of the Last Supper in Matthew (26:17), Mark (14:12), and Luke (22:7-8) is the same. All references indicate that Jesus sent his disciples to make preparations for the Passover meal that they were going to eat together.

Matthew 26:17		Now on the first day of Unleavened Bread the disciples came to Jesus, saying "Where will you have us prepare for you to eat the Passover?"
Mark 14:12		And on the first day of Unleavened Bread, when they sacrificed the Passover lamb, his disciples said to him, "where will you have us go and prepare for you to eat the Passover?"
Luke 22:7-8		They came the day of Unleavened Bread, on which the Passover lamb had to be sacrificed. So Jesus sent Peter and John, saying, "Go and prepare the Passover for us that we may eat."

2. Jesus Ate With His Twelve Disciples

From the gospel accounts (Matthew 26:20; Mark 14:17-18; Luke 22:14-15) it seems apparent that Jesus ate his supper with his twelve disciples. Matthew and Mark's accounts are clearer on this point than Luke's. Matthew, Mark and Luke's accounts affirm that it is Jesus and his twelve disciples who ate this supper. Nothing is mentioned about any women being present. The traditional quorum of ten men was observed by Jesus at this meal.

Matthew 26:20		When it was evening, he sat at table with the twelve disciples; as they were eating...
Mark 14:17-18		And when it was evening he came with the twelve. And as they were at table eating...
Luke 22:14-15		And when the hour came, he sat at table, and the apostles with him. And he said to them, "I have earnestly desired to eat this passover with you before I suffer."

3. Jesus' Words Over the Bread

The gospel accounts (Matthew 26:26; Mark 14:22; Luke 22:19-20) indicate that Jesus blessed the bread and said certain words over it. The Matthew and Mark accounts give the blessing of the bread first, but the Luke account gives the blessing of the bread after the first blessing of the wine. At the traditional Passover meal, the symbolism of the food was explained by the father or leader. At Jesus' Last Supper, he gives a different meaning to the bread than the traditional Passover meal, relating the bread to his own body.

Matthew 26:26   Now as they were eating, Jesus took bread, and blessed, and broke it, and gave it to the disciples and said, "take, eat; this is my body."

Mark 14:22   And as they were eating, he took bread, and blessed and broke it, and gave it to them and said, "take; this is my body."

Luke 22:19-20   And he took bread and when he had given thanks he broke it and gave it to them saying: "this is my body."

4. Jesus' Words Over the Wine

The gospel accounts (Matthew 26:27-28; Mark 14:23-24; Luke 22:17-20) record the words of Jesus over the wine. Matthew's and Mark's accounts indicate that the wine is Jesus' blood, which is related to the covenant idea and is shed for many. Matthew alone mentions that the expiatory effect of Jesus' blood is for the remission of sins. Luke's account relates that Jesus' blood is "shed for you." Finally, Matthew's and Mark's gospels do not give any indication of the time of the blessing after the meal.

Matthew 26:27-28		And he took a cup, and when he had given thanks he gave it to them saying, "Drink of it all of you, for this is my blood of the covenant, which is poured out for many for the foregiveness of sins."
Mark 14:23-24		And he took a cup and when he had given thanks he gave it to them and they all drank of it. And he said to them, "this is my blood of the covenant, which is poured out for many."
Luke 22:17-20		And he took a cup and when he had given thanks he said, "Take this and divide it among yourselves; for I tell you that from now on I shall not drink of the fruit of the vine until the kingdom of God comes." And he took bread, and when he had given thanks he broke it and gave it to them, saying, "This is my body."

5. Jesus' Last Supper in Relation to the Establishment of the Kingdom

All three synoptic accounts (Matthew 26:29; Mark 14:25; Luke 22:16, 18) record Jesus' vow of abstinence which was to be in force until the eschatological coming of the Kingdom of God. Matthew and Mark mention the vow only once. Luke, however, records the vow twice. Jesus' vow is mentioned before the blessing of the bread and wine in relation to Passover itself. Again, Luke mentions Jesus' vow when he first blesses the cup of wine and gives it to them to drink. It seems, therefore, that Matthew and Mark describe Jesus' Last Supper as the last step in the final phase of the establishment of the Kingdom of God and as the anticipated fulfillment of the Messianic Banquet. Luke indicates that the eschatological fulfillment of the Kingdom of God has already taken place with Jesus' Last Supper. In conclusion, then, it seems all three synoptic accounts record Jesus' Last Supper as an anticipated Messianic Banquet.

Matthew 26:29   I tell you I shall not drink again of this fruit of the vine until that day when I drink it new with you in my Father's kingdom.

Mark 14:25   Truly, I say to you, I shall not drink again of the fruit of the vine until that day when I drink it new in the kingdom of God.

Luke 22:16   For I tell you that I shall not eat it until it is fulfilled in the kingdom of God.

Luke 22:18   For I tell you that from now on I shall not drink until the Kingdom of God comes.

In conclusion, the synoptic accounts reveal the following points:

1. All three synoptic accounts record Jesus' actions; he blessed, broke, and gave bread to his disciples. (Matthew 26:26; Mark 14:22; Luke 22:19-20)

2. All three synoptic accounts record that Jesus says the bread he blessed is his body. Luke mentions that Jesus says his body will be given for them, whereas Matthew and Mark say that it will be given "for many." (Matthew 26:26; Mark 14:22; Luke 22:19-20).

3. It is only in Luke's account that one finds that Jesus commanded a reenactment of what he did over the bread and wine. (Luke 22:19-20)

4. All three synoptic accounts record that Jesus blessed the wine and says that it is his blood. Luke's account mentions only the new covenant idea. (Matthew 26:27-28; Mark 14:23-24; Luke 17-20).

5. Matthew mentions that Jesus invited his disciples to eat and drink; Mark mentions the invitation to eat and Luke omits the invitation to eat and drink. (Matthew 26:27-28; Mark 14:23-24)

6. Mark's account observes that all drink of the cup. Matthew and Luke are silent on this point. (Mark 14:23-24)

7. Matthew and Mark, like Luke, do not explicitly say that Jesus himself ate with his disciples, but it is clear that he was the host at the supper. (Matthew 26:27-28; Mark 14:23-24; Luke 22:17-20)

8. Neither Matthew, Mark nor Luke mentions that Jesus and his disciples ate the roasted lamb. (Matthew 26:26-28; Mark 14:22-24; Luke 22:7-8)

9. Matthew's account mentions that Jesus said, "In my Father's kingdom." (Matthew 26:29) However, Mark (14:25) and Luke (22:16) say "in the kingdom of God."

INTERPRETATION OF TERMS BREAD AND WINE

The Synoptic Gospels relate that Jesus used bread and wine at the Last Supper. They also say that he said a blessing at the meal and he referred to the bread as his body and to the wine as his blood of the covenant. Briefly, an examination of the meaning of these words will be made.

Jesus used bread at the Last Supper according to the synoptic writings. The question is what type of bread was used? Scholars like Von Allmen,[122] Steinmueller[123] and M'Clintock and Strong[124] believe that Jesus used unleavened bread. Allen[125] maintains that it was probably unleavened bread. Hastings[126] says that it was probably ordinary bread. Then, there are scholars like Jeremias[127] and Shepherd[128] who say that the word for bread in Hebrew, Lehem, can be used for leavened or unleavened bread. Unleavened bread as distinguished from ordinary bread (leavened bread) was made from water and flour of wheat, rye, barley, oats or spelt.[129]

The scholars who favor the unleavened bread idea reason that except for religious reasons, unleavened bread was prepared only when the occasion demanded great haste.

(Genesis 18:6; Exodus 12:34; Judges 6:19) But in the liturgy, in the Feast of Passover, leavened bread was forbidden by biblical prescriptions. (Exodus 23:18; 34:25; Leviticus 2:4-11)

Delorme[130] is not sure what type of bread Jesus used at the meal. However, there are some scholars[131] who say that the word, bread, in Hebrew could also mean food. Therefore, they claim it is not certain that Jesus used bread at all.

The synoptic accounts (Matthew 26:26; Mark 14:22; Luke 22:19) record that Jesus blessed bread. It is reasonable to assume that bread and not some other type of food was blessed by Jesus. Likewise, Brownlee's and Vermes' translations of the Qumranian sacred meal (MD 6:2-8; VMR 2:11-22) indicate that bread was blessed by the priest.

The synoptics say that Jesus not only used bread, but he broke the bread and gave it to his disciples. What did the breaking of the bread mean? According to Delorme,[132] the breaking of the bread was one of the essential parts of any Jewish meal. Jeremias,[133] Conzelmann[134] and Kuhn[135] agree with Delorme. The breaking of bread was an ancient custom of Palestine and was done at ordinary family meals, special meals with guests, Passover meals, and Kiddush meals.[136] Therefore, it seems that Jesus followed a customary practice for eating together.

In addition to the bread being used by Jesus, the Synoptic Gospels relate that Jesus used wine at the meal. What type of wine was used? Higgins[137] and others[138] believe that it was red wine. Von Allmen[139] agrees but adds that it apparently was diluted with a little water. Schweizer[140] and others[141] believe that wine was used but they are not certain of the color or whether it was mixed with water. These scholars say that Jesus used wine at the Last Supper because it was a Passover meal. One of the prescriptions for the Passover meal was that four cups of wine were to be used at the liturgy.

According to the synoptic writings, Jesus blessed the bread and wine at the Last Supper. It was customary for Jews to have a blessing before and after ordinary meals.[142]

Zeitlin[143] says that it was a common practice among Jews to bless God before a meal, and if a priest was present he would do it. Beyer[144] says it was a rule that nothing should be eaten before a blessing was given. Blessing before meals was an ancient custom but it became more formal during Rabbinic times.[145] Not only were the ordinary Jewish meals blessed before they were eaten but also the special evening meal in preparation for the Sabbath or a feast day.[146] At Jewish meals, the head of the house, or the priest, if present, took a loaf of bread, spoke a blessing, broke the bread and gave a piece to each one sitting at the table, so that by eating the bread, each might share the blessing. The same procedure was followed for the drinking of wine, though the wine was usually confined to special occasions of festivity or mourning. In general, then, Jewish meals, whether partaken alone or with a family or group of friends, had religious significance, since a formal blessing was offered to God over bread and wine. Apparently, Jesus followed the normal custom when he blessed the bread and wine at the Last Supper. He was not necessarily following a custom peculiar to the Jewish people at Qumran.

BIBLICAL SCHOLARS' OPINIONS

Scholars have interpreted the synoptic passages that recount Jesus' Last Supper in various ways.

1. The Last Supper Was Simply an Ordinary Jewish Meal

Driver[147] and Rowley[148] believe that Jesus celebrated his last meal with his disciples. They say that it was an ordinary meal but his impending death gave it a special meaning. Anderson[149] agrees with these two scholars and emphatically disagrees with the idea that Jesus' Last Supper was a Passover meal or any special meal such as a Kiddush. Likewise, Wilson[150] agrees with Anderson. Brilioth[151] quotes Bauer and Renan's opinion that the Last Supper was just an ordinary Jewish meal but believes that Jesus' disciples gave it a special meaning.

2. The Last Supper Was a Kiddush Meal

Both Brilioth[152] and Box[153] say that the Last Supper was a Kiddush meal. The Kiddush, or santification of the day, was a blessing which was said at the beginning or during the meal on the eve of the Sabbath or any feast day.[154] In general, a group of men would gather in the afternoon to read and study the Torah, exchange comments on the Scriptures and then offer a prayer of thanks to God before partaking of bread and wine during a simple meal together. At the meal, the Kiddush (blessing) would usually be said over the cup of wine but if there was no wine the blessing would be said over the bread. The Kiddush, or weekly santification of the Sabbath, goes back to pre-Christian times. It is not confined to the santification of the Sabbath alone but also to great feasts, such as Passover, Pentecost, and Tabernacles.[155]

3. The Last Supper Was a Fellowship Meal Which Will be Completed in the Future

At the present time, a few scholars such as Kilmartin,[156] hold the opinion that Jesus' Last Supper was a fellowship meal which started a new era that would be completed in the future. Klausner[157] says that, in his opinion, Jesus' disciples believed he had celebrated the Passover meal before his arrest and he had commanded that they institute a fellowship meal in his memory. Furthermore, he believes that Jesus himself did not institute the fellowship meal but his disciples, at a later time, did eat fellowship meals, at which time they recalled the practices and words of Jesus.[158] If Jesus' Last Supper was a fellowship meal, then it may have been similar to the fellowship meals of the Pharisaic Jew of his time. The Pharisees had these meals in their Guilds or Haburoth.[159] The Haburoth consisted of associations of pious Jews who kept aloof from common men so that they would not contract any form of impurity. They assembled for meals that usually followed the pattern of the Passover celebration. Although many Pharisees were members of the Haburoth, not all were.[160] Because of the paucity of information concerning the practices and customs of the Haburoth fellowship meals, it is difficult to compare Jesus' Last Supper with these meals. In fact, the chief source of such information comes from later Rabbinic sources, and they usually mention only special occasions such as weddings, funerals, and circumcisions.[161]

4. The Last Supper Was an Eschatological Meal in
Anticipation of the Messianic Banquet

Scholars such as Finegan,[162] McKenzie,[163] Dodd,[164] Marxsen,[165] and Allen[166] believe that Jesus' Last Supper was a meal that anticipated a Messianic banquet to be celebrated in heaven. Davies[167] agrees with these scholars but adds that Jesus essentially followed the manner in which the Qumran sacred meal was partaken. They claim that the cup of wine Jesus shared with his followers was a symbol and a pledge of the cup he would share with them at the next banquet in the Messianic kingdom.

5. The Last Supper Was a Farewell Meal

Yet, there are scholars[168] who hold that the Last Supper was a farewell meal within the setting of the Passover meal, which anticipated the eschatological meal to be eaten in the Kingdom. Other scholars, such as Schweizer,[169] say that the Last Supper was a farewell meal similar to the farewell meals of the dying Patriarchs. These were eaten in anticipation of the Messianic Banquet to come. Then, scholars like Bundy[170] and Delorme[171] hold the theory that the Last Supper of Jesus was simply a farewell meal.

6. The Last Supper Was a Passover Meal

Many scholars favor the theory that Jesus' Last Supper was a Passover meal. In particular, Kallas,[172] Jeremias,[173] Harrison,[174] Higgins,[175] Anderson,[176] and Allbright[177] support the Passover theory. These scholars state that Jesus' Last Supper was a Passover meal because it fulfilled the requirements of the Seder of the first night of Passover. The bread that Jesus ate was unleavened and the wine that was used by the Jews on the first night of Passover. The humn sung by Jesus and his followers after the meal was the Hallel which is sung by the Jews on that night. Leehardt[178] believes that Jesus' Last Supper was a Passover meal but that He introduced an innovation at his supper. Jesus gave a new interpretation to the bread and wine. He said the bread was his body, and the wine was his blood. Ruchstuhl[179] and Kallas[180] say that Jesus' Last Supper was probably a Passover meal. Benoit[181] called Jesus' meal a Passover meal, a Messianic meal, an alliance meal that anticipated an eschatological meal.

The answer to the question of whether Jesus' Last Supper was a Passover meal depends partially on the calendar used by Jesus and his followers. In brief, the Dead Sea Scrolls reveal that the Qumranians probably followed the solar calendar and not the official Jewish calendar of Jesus' time.[182] Did Jesus follow the official Jewish calendar or the Qumranian calendar? Men like Danielou,[183] Stauffer,[184] Sutcliffe,[185] and Allen[186] believe that Jesus may have followed the Qumranian calendar which celebrated the Passover meal on Tuesday and not Thursday. Since there is evidence from the Dead Sea Scrolls that the solar calendar was used by the Qumranians, these scholars argue that the Qumranians would have followed the solar calendar since it was older than the lunar calendar. Therefore, Jesus may have been aware of this solar calendar and followed it. As a result of this solar calendar Jesus would have celebrated the Passover on a day different from the lunar calendar of the Jerusalem priesthood. There is evidence that during the last pre-Christian centuries certain groups among the Jews followed the solar calendar which was so arranged that the various religious feasts of the year were fixed on certain days of the month.[187] However, it has been stated that one cannot assume the Qumranians actually used the solar calendar, despite the rather convincing evidence that they did.[188] It is at least problematical that the Qumranians used this calendar.[189] It is possible that the sect actually followed the solar calendar for a short period. The evidence on the actual use of the calendar remains contradictory and inconclusive. Schubert[190] says that there is no indication that Jesus and his disciples followed the Qumranian calendar instead of the official Jewish calendar. The evidence is insufficient to prove that Jesus followed the Qumranian calendar. Therefore, the question as to whether Jesus celebrated an authentic Passover meal at the Last Supper still remains unsettled.

7. The Last Supper Was a Meal Within the Framework of the Passover

There are scholars[191] who believe that the Last Supper was probably an ordinary meal, if it was not a Passover celebration, set within the framework of the Passover meal.

However, Shepherd[192] says that the Last Supper would have been linked with Eschatological expectations. Although the Last Supper was probably not a Passover meal, it was a religious meal similar to a Passover meal.[193]

8. The Last Supper Was Not a Passover Meal

Some scholars[194] doubt whether the Last Supper of Jesus was a Passover meal. The scholars who doubt or deny that the Last Supper was a Passover meal state that the Synoptic Gospels' account of the Last Supper does not make any reference to the Passover meal, the chief feature of which was the eating of the Passover lamb. Some authorities[195] claim that Jesus' Last Supper had a setting midway between a Passover meal and the anticipated eschatological Messianic banquet.

In view of the many interpretations regarding the Last Supper, there is no consensus. The synoptic writers claim that Jesus did celebrate a Passover meal at the Last Supper. Yet all do not agree. The Last Supper may or may not have been a Passover meal, but the evidence has not been strong enough to prove that it was. Therefore, it seems that Jesus' Last Supper was probably a religious meal with eschatological anticipations similar to other religious meals of his time. His supper was not necessarily an imitation of the Qumranian sacred meal. He may have modeled his supper on other religious meals, such as the Passover, fellowship, and farewell meals which were contemporary with the Qumranian sacred meals.

JESUS' POSSIBLE CONTACT WITH QUMRAN

Since the Synoptic Gospels speak of Jesus' being in contact with John the Baptist, who may have been in contact with the Qumran community, Benoit,[196] Davies,[197] and Larson[198] believe that Jesus may have been a member of the Qumran community or at least in some way connected with them.

Allegro[199] and Vermes[200] say that it is highly improbable Jesus was a member of the Qumran community. Even if Jesus' Last Supper were connected with an eschatological banquet like the Qumran sacred meals, there are notable differences such as the interpretation attached to the bread and wine and the seating arrangement at the meal.[201] McKenzie[202] and Milik[203] agree with Allegro. Rowley,[204] Zeitlin,[205] Jeremias,[206] Burrows,[207] Smyth,[208] and Driver[209] state that Jesus' Last Supper was not influenced at all by the Qumranian sacred meals. Yet, scholars like Groh[210] and Kuhn[211] claim a definite relationship between Jesus' meal and the Qumranian sacred meals.

Scholars such as Black,[212] Harrison,[213] Ringgren,[214] Bruce[215] and Gordon,[216] point out the similarities between Jesus' Last Supper and the Qumranian sacred meals. These similarities are the bread and wine, the blessing, and the eschatological significance. Stauffer,[217] claims that these similarities may be accounted for by the direct or indirect influence of Qumran on Jesus. Qumran is the spiritual home of Jesus.

However, there are scholars like Danielou [218] and Brown[219] who are not certain whether Jesus was influenced by Qumranian religious practices. LaSor[220] believes that Jesus' Last Supper was influenced by the Passover meals, not the Qumranian meals. Carmignac[221] and Rowley [222] agree with LaSor, except they say the Last Supper of Jesus was influenced by ordinary Jewish meals. Unlike some scholars, Higgins[223] believes that the Last Supper of Jesus had very strong resemblances to the Qumranian sacred meals. Teicher[224] claims that Jesus may have been influenced by Qumranian thinking, since some of Jesus' sayings in Mark's gospel (10:6) have been discovered in Dead Sea literature.

Hjerl-Hansen [225] says it seems improbable that, if Jesus stayed in the desert for a period of time, he would not have sought contact with the Qumran people living in the same desert. If that happened, then there is the possibility that Jesus may have been influenced by the Qumranian religious practices, especially their sacred meals.

It appears the evidence is not clear that Jesus was a member of the Qumran community. However, there does seem to be more evidence of some sort of Qumranian influence on him.

SUMMARY

The synoptic accounts say very little about Jesus' childhood and adolescence. They speak of his adulthood in terms of his ministry in Galilee of Palestine.

All three synoptic accounts, however, narrate the Last Supper of Jesus. They say that it took place during the Passover. Matthew and Mark state that it was a Passover meal while Luke does not specifically call it a Passover meal. Biblical scholars are not in agreement that it was a Passover meal. Those who do not believe it was a Passover meal say that certain features of a traditional Passover meal are missing from the synoptic accounts. For instance, the synoptic accounts say nothing about the killing of the lamb at the Temple, the roasting and eating of it, the unleavened bread, and the bitter herbs or sauce. These scholars also note that the synoptic accounts do not say that Jesus ate the meal with his disciples.

Although all three accounts mention that Jesus blessed the bread and wine, broke the bread and distributed it to those at the Supper, the chronological sequence of these events is not identical. The synoptic accounts seem to stress the remembrance of Jesus, a new covenant, his sacrifice for man, and finally an eschatological hope that all of them will again be united.

Since the synoptic writers speak of Jesus associating with John the Baptist who may have been in contact with the Qumran community, scholars such as Benoit, Larson, and Davies believe that Jesus may have known the Qumranian community. Although scholars, among whom are Vermes and Allegro, deny the probability of Jesus being an actual member of the Qumran community, they do not deny the possibility of his having some contact with them. The biblical scholars, Rowley, Jeremias, Burrows and others, do not believe that Jesus modeled his Last Supper on the Qumranian sacred meal. However, there are others, such as Groh and Kuhn, who believe that the Last Supper shows signs of Qumranian influence. There are similarities such as the elements of bread and wine, the blessing and eschatological significance between Jesus' Last Supper and the Qumranian sacred meal.

Yet these similarities can also be found in the fellowship meals, farewell meals, Kiddush meals, and Passover meals during Jesus' time. Therefore, Jesus, in planning his Last Supper, was not necessarily influenced by the Qumranian sacred meals but perhaps by these other religious meals, and the forces of his impending agony, sacrifice and destiny.

Although it seems impossible at the present time to prove that Jesus was a member of the Qumranian community, it is possible to say that he may have been influenced by some of the Qumranian customs regarding their sacred meal. Furthermore, there is no likelihood that Jesus was ever a member of the Qumran community. However, it seems improbable that Jesus, who traveled throughout Palestine, was unaware of the religious practices of the Qumranians who were a very religious group of Jews. Since the information about Jesus' Last Supper, as well as that of the Qumranian sacred meal, is scanty, it seems at least probable that Jesus could have followed some of the Qumranian customs in preparing the Last Supper. Yet, the Qumranian sacred meal probably was not the sole influence on Jesus, since there were other religious meals, such as the Kiddush, Passover, fellowship and farewell meals, during the time of his ministry in Palestin.

CHAPTER IV

COMPARISONS AND CONCLUSIONS

From the data that has been collected some comparisons and conclusions are possible.

Comparisons

From the synoptic accounts, the material about Jesus' childhood and adolescence is scanty. He was born in Bethlehem, five miles south of Jerusalem, in Palestine, during the reign of Herod the Great. During his lifetime, he preached chiefly in Galilee. He was a contemporary of John the Baptist and the Qumranians. During the last week of his life, he celebrated his Last Supper with his most intimate friends in Jerusalem.

The elements of his supper have suggested to some scholars a possible connection with the Qumranian sacred meal. I've compared the Last Supper with the Qumranians' sacred meal under these categories.

1. Formula

Neither the Manual of Discipline (6:2-8) nor the Messianic Rule Fragment (2:11-22) indicates that a formula was used at the Qumranian meals. The Manual of Discipline (6:5-6 B.V.) says, "The priest shall first stretch out his hand to invoke a blessing with the first of the bread and wine." In the Messianic Rule Fragment (2:11-22 V.V.), it states, "Let no man extend his hand over the first fruits of bread and wine before the priest." The Messianic Rule Fragment (2:11-22) describes the same procedure as outlined in the Manual of Discipline (6:2-8) but adds that if the Messiah of Israel is present, then he will bless the bread after the priest. These two documents specify the arrangement according to rank, and the order or procedure. The priest would say the traditional Jewish blessing for the bread and/or wine. There is no indication that the priest or anyone else used a certain expression when they were assembled for these meals. What were these meals? The translations themselves do not give an answer to the question. Scholars have speculated as to whether the <u>Manual of Discipline</u> (6:2-8) refers to the Qumranian daily common meals, special festive meals, or a future Messianic Banquet. There is debate whether the <u>Messianic Rule Fragment</u> (2:11-22) refers to a future Messianic banquet or a regular meal with certain procedures to be observed if the Messiah or Messiahs arrived. Scholars do not agree on whether the <u>Manual of Discipline</u> (6:2-8) and the <u>Messianic Rule Fragment</u> (2:11-22) were originally one document.

On the other hand, the Synoptic Gospels (Matthew 26:26; Mark 14:22; Luke 22:19-20) record the words of Jesus at his Last Supper. Matthew's account (26:26) states, Now as they were eating, Jesus took bread, blessed and broke it, and gave it to the disciples and said, "take and eat; this is my body." Again, Matthew (26:27-28) says, And he took a cup, and when he had given thanks, saying "Drink of it all of you, for this is my blood of the covenant which is poured out for many for the forgiveness of sins." Both Mark (14:17-24) and Luke (22:14-20) record similar accounts of Jesus' words over the bread and wine. Jesus compares the bread to his body and the wine to his blood. There is nothing similar to it in the translations of the Qumran <u>Manual of Discipline</u> or the <u>Messianic Rule Fragment</u>. Scholars, with the exception of Davies, do not see the bread and wine at the Qumranian meals being compared to the body and blood of the Messiah or Messiahs. A final point is that the Gospel of Luke (22:20) records that Jesus commanded that his actions be repeated. Luke (22:20) states, "Do this as a memorial of me." Once again, there is no evidence of a similar command in the Qumranian meals by the priest, Messiah or Messiahs, or anyone else.

2. <u>Words</u> - "Priest"; "Communal"; "Rank"; "Eat"; "Drink"; "Bread"; "Wine"

The <u>Manual of Discipline</u> (6:3-6 B.V.) states, "And in every place where there are ten men of the council of the Community, there shall not cease from among them a man who is a priest. And let each one according to his assigned position or rank sit before him. And it shall be when they arrange the table to eat, the priest shall first stretch out his hand to invoke a blessing with the first of the bread and wine." The <u>Messianic Rule Fragment</u> (2:11-22) indicates that the priest will bless the bread before anyone eats. In these documents, it is clear that the priest had an important function at the Qumranian meals.

On the other hand, there is no priest present at the Last Supper of Jesus. Jesus, even though he was not a priest, blessed the bread and wine. In the same way as the accounts of Matthew (26:26-28) and Luke (22:14-20), Mark (14:22-24) states, And as they were eating, he took bread and blessed and broke it, and gave it to them and said, "Take; this is my body." And he took a cup and when he had given thanks he gave it to them and they all drank of it. And he said to them, "This is my blood of the covenant, which is poured out for many." Therefore, it is Jesus who blesses the bread and wine at his meal. At the Qumranian meals, it is the priest who blesses the bread and wine.

Another feature of the Qumranian meals was that they ate communally. The Manual of Discipline (6:2 B.V.) says, "they shall eat communally, and bless communally, and take counsel communally." At the Last Supper of Jesus, it is apparent that it was a very special meal and so a selected number of disciples were invited. Mark's account (14:17-18) states, "And when it was evening he came with the twelve, and as they were at table eating." However, they did eat communally, as did the Qumranians.

What about the arrangement at the meal? The Qumranians observed procedures of rank at their meals. The Manual of Discipline (6:4 B.V.) states "And let each one according to his assigned position or rank sit before him." The synoptic accounts of Jesus' Last Supper do not indicate whether Jesus' disciples sat according to rank.

Did the Qumranians eat a meal at which the bread and wine were part of it? It seems highly probable that the Qumranians did. The Manual of Discipline (6:4-5 B.V.) states, "And it shall be when they arrange the table to eat." It was customary at Jewish meals to bless the bread. Wine was present usually at festive meals or special meals.

The synoptic accounts (Matthew 26:20; Mark 14:17-18; Luke 22:14-15) record that the disciples were at table and ate. They do not say whether or not Jesus ate with his disciples. It seems probable that Jesus ate a meal with his disciples. Once again, bread and wine were most likely present since it was a very special meal. It was Jesus' last meal on earth and he was to give his farewell discourse at it.

Another similarity between the Qumran meals and Jesus' Last Supper was the bread and wine. The Manual of Discipline

(6:5-6 B.V.) says, "The priest shall first stretch out his hand to invoke a blessing with the first of the bread and wine." The Synoptic Gospels state that Jesus blessed the bread and wine at the meal. For example, Matthew (26:26-28) states, Now as they were eating, Jesus took bread, and blessed and broke it, and gave it to the disciples and said, "take and eat, this is my body." And he took a cup, and when he had given thanks he gave it to them saying, "Drink of it all of you, for this is my blood of the covenant which is poured out for many for the forgiveness of sins." Although there is disagreement as to the type of bread and wine at the Qumranian meals and Jesus' Last Supper, it is generally agreed that they were used. What is significantly different between the Qumranian meals and Jesus' Last Supper is the interpretation that Jesus gave to the bread and wine. Did he actually mean that the bread is his body and the wine his blood? Was it a metaphorical or symbolic saying of Jesus? Although scholars differ as to the actual intention of Jesus, it is clear that he associated a special meaning with the bread and wine. Partaking of the bread and wine, Jesus' disciples apparently shared in his body and blood. There is no parallel in the Qumranian Manual of Discipline and the Messianic Rule Fragment. Jesus is unique in this point of comparison.

3. <u>Words</u>.- "Bless"; "Men"; "Messiah of Israel"

At the Qumranian meals, it was the priest who blessed the bread and wine. The Manual of Discipline (6:5-6 B.V.) states, "The priest shall first stretch out his hand to invoke a blessing with the first of the bread and the wine." The Messianic Rule Fragment (2:11-22 V.V.) states, "Let no man extend his hand over the first fruits of bread and wine before the priest." On the contrary, it was Jesus who blessed the bread and wine at his Last Supper. Jesus did not follow the ordinary Jewish blessings at meal, for it was customary for the father of the family to bless the bread and to have a guest bless the wine. According to the synoptic accounts, Jesus gave both blessings. Jesus' approach was more that of a leader of the group than that of a father of a family. And so, Jesus did not follow the practice of Qumran nor the traditional Jewish practice at His Last Supper.

According to the Manual of Discipline (6:3-4), only men took part in the meals. However, the Manual of Discipline (6:3 B.V.) states, "They shall eat communally, and bless communally, and take counsel communally." There is archeological evidence that women lived at Qumran. Were these women permitted to attend these meals? Although the Manual of Discipline (6:2-8) and the Messianic Rule Fragment (2:11-22) do not specifically say that women were present at these meals, it can be reasonably assumed that they were.

Likewise, the synoptic accounts (Matthew 26:20; Mark 14:17-18; Luke 22:14-15) indicate that Jesus ate his last meal with his twelve disciples. For example, Matthew (26:20) states, "When it was evening, he sat at table with the twelve disciples; as they were eating." Is it possible that some women were present at Jesus' Last Supper? It is possible but most improbable. His Last Supper was to have special significance for his disciples. Therefore, the Last Supper was probably limited just to his twelve special followers. But, on other occasions such as the marriage feast of Cana, Jesus ate with all types of people. This was contrary to the practice at Qumran. They ate with only the "clean" people. Strictly speaking, according to the synoptic accounts and the Qumranian documents, men only were present at the Last Supper as well as at the Qumran meals.

A final point to be considered is the phrase "Messiah of Israel." This expression is found only in the Qumranian Messianic Rule Fragment (2:11-22). It read, "And then the Messiah of Israel shall come, and the chiefs of the clans of Israel shall sit before him." There is no mention of the "Messiah of Israel" in the Manual of Discipline. (6:2-8) However, it is possible that at one time these two documents were one single account. Nevertheless, if the "Messiah of Israel" came, the Qumranians had made provision for his place at the meal. He would give a blessing following the blessing of the priest. The problem arises did the Qumranians expect one or two Messiahs? There is no clear answer since translations of the Messianic Rule Fragment (2:11-22) give different indications. For example, Vermes' translation of the Messianic Rule Fragment (2:11-22) indicates that there would be two Messiahs, a lay person and a priest. In either case, it seems fairly certain that the Qumranians expected at least one Messiah.

On the other hand, the synoptic accounts contain no expression parallel to the Messiah of Israel. If Jesus' disciples considered Him a Messiah, it is not stated in the synoptic accounts of the Last Supper of Jesus.

4. Theological Significance

The Qumranian sacred meal and Jesus' Last Supper have a parallel in the breaking of bread, which was an essential part of any Jewish meal, not exclusive to the Qumranian meals. The breaking of bread was an ancient Jewish custom at ordinary family meals, special meals with guests, Passover meals, and Kiddush meals. Therefore, it seems that Jesus followed a practice that was customary when eating with others. The Qumranians, like other Jews, probably did the same thing.

What does seem significantly different is the interpretation that Jesus gave to the bread and wine. According to the synoptic writings, he used these elements as symbols of his body and blood, in the light of his impending death. It is this fact that gives special meaning to his use of the bread and wine. Even as everyone present at the meal ate the bread and drank the wine, so would they all share in the atonement of his death, of his body and his blood to be shed.

This understanding of the bread and wine at the Last Supper pointing to the death of Jesus is not paralleled at Qumran. It is impossible to avoid this interpretive significance, which can be traced back to Jesus Himself. There is no such theological significance given to the Qumran sacred meal. In the final analysis, it is the person of Jesus that makes his meal significantly different from the Qumran sacred meal. It might be added that any coincidental resemblance between the Qumranian sacred meal and Jesus' Last Supper might be the common descent of both from the rite of Passover.

Conclusions

The importance of the Manual of Discipline, the Messianic Rule Fragment and the Synoptic Gospels needs no emphasis. The Manual of Discipline describes the Qumranian baptismal practices. The Manual of Discipline and the Messianic Rule Fragment discuss the Qumranian meals. One may refer to them as "sacred" in the sense that every Jewish meal was sacred because it was blessed. On the other hand, the synoptic accounts relate the Last Supper of Jesus. From these writings, it is possible to reconstruct the religious rites and practices of the Qumranians, and Jesus.

It is recorded in the synoptic writings that Jesus used certain expressions that he desired his followers to use. There is no such evidence in the Qumranian literature that either the Teacher of Righteousness or any other person left a set formula for future generations to repeat. These two meals resembled one another in so far as the same elements of bread and wine were partaken, and a blessing at the meals was given. They differed in that Jesus, who was not a priest, blessed the elements. It was the priest who blessed the bread and wine at the Qumranian meals. The principal difference between these meals was Jesus. It was his Last Supper. Because of his imminent death, he designated the bread and wine as symbols of his body and blood. It was a reminder to his followers that every time they gather to eat the bread and drink the wine, they are sharing in his sacrifice. Therefore, the basic and comprehensive difference is in Jesus and his meaning for his followers.

In final conclusion, I would like to add the following points: First, the Qumran and Synoptic literature have a different historical aim. They seem to be in different circles since not a single person, date, or event is mentioned in common in both sets of literature. Second, the two bodies of literature are similar in religious aims. Both have come from sectarian movements in Judaism, sharing eschatological expectations. Third, the Dead Sea Scrolls provide valuable material for the study of sectarian Judaism as Christianity arose. Besides normative Judaism, there now exists scrolls from Qumran as a background for the study of the birth of Christianity. The Qumranians were deeply religious Jews who were searching for God. I can find no better way to conclude than to quote Burrows' statement: "It is as though Jesus and they (Qumran) drew water from the same spring but carried it in different vessels."[226]

APPENDIX

MANUAL OF DISCIPLINE

William Brownlee's Translation of the Manual of Discipline[1]

Chapter 6:2-6

In these (regulations) let them walk in
all their dwellings, everyone who is present,
each with his fellow. The lesser shall obey
the greater, in regard to goods and means.
They shall eat communally, and bless
communally, and take counsel communally; and in
every place where there are ten men of the
council of the Community, there shall not
cease from among them a man who is priest.
And let each one according to his assigned
position (or rank) sit before him; and in
that order let them be asked for their
counsel with regard to every matter. And it
shall be when they arrange the table to eat,
or (arrange) the wine to drink, the priest
shall first stretch out his hand to invoke
a blessing with the first of the bread or
the wine to drink, the priest shall first
stretch out his hand to invoke a blessing
with the first of the bread and the wine.

Geza Vermes' Translation of the Manual of Discipline[1]

Chapter 6:2-6

These are the ways in which all of them
shall walk, each man with his companion,
wherever they dwell.

---

[1]Brownlee, The Dead Sea Manual of Discipline, 22.
[1]Vermes, The Dead Sea Scrolls in English, 80-81.

The man of lesser rank shall obey the
greater in matters of work and money.

They shall eat in common and pray in
common and deliberate in common.

Wherever there are ten men of the Council
of the Community there shall not lack a
Priest among them. And they shall all sit
before him according to their rank and
shall be asked their counsel in all things
in that order. And when the table has been
prepared for eating, and the new wine for
drinking, the Priest shall be the first
to stretch out his hand to bless the first-
fruits of the bread and new wine.

Geza Vermes' Translation of the Messianic Rule Fragment[1]

Chapter 2:11-22

He shall come at the head of the whole
congregation of Israel with all his
brethren, the sons of Aaron the Priests,
those called to the assembly, the men of
renown; and they shall sit before him, each
man in the order of his dignity. And then
the Messiah of Israel shall come, and the
chiefs of the clans of Israel shall sit
before him, each in the order of his
dignity, according to his place in their
camps and marches. And before them shall
sit all the heads of family of the
congregation, and the wise men of the holy
congregation, each in the order of his
dignity.

And when they shall gather for the common
table, to eat and to drink new wine, when
the common table shall be set for eating

---

[1]Vermes, *The Dead Sea Scrolls in English*, 121.

and the new wine poured for drinking, let
no man extend his hand over the first-
fruits of bread and wine before the Priest;
for it is he who shall bless the first-
fruits of bread and wine, and shall be
the first to extend his hand over the
bread. Thereafter, the Messiah of Israel
shall extend his hand over the bread,
and all the Congregation of the Community
shall utter a blessing, each man in the
order of his dignity.

It is according to this statute that
they shall proceed at every meal at
which at least ten men are gathered
together.

Revised Standard Version Translation of the Synoptic Gospels Account of Jesus' Last Supper[1]

Matthew 26:17-29

17   Now on the first day of Unleavened Bread the disciples came to Jesus saying, "Where will you have us prepare for you to eat the passover?"

18   He said, "Go into the city to such a one, and say to him, 'The Teacher says, My time is at hand; I will keep the passover at your house with my disciples'."

19   And the disciples did as Jesus had directed them, and they prepared the passover.

20   When it was evening, he sat at table with the twelve disciples;

21   and as they were eating, he said, "Truly, I say to you, one of you will betray me."

22   And they were very sorrowful, and began to say to him one after another, "Is it I, Lord?"

23   He answered, "He who has dipped his hand in the dish with me, will betray me.

24   The Son of man goes as it is written of him, but woe to that man by whom the Son of man is betrayed! It would have been better for that man if he had not been born."

25   Judas, who betrayed him, said, "Is it I, Master?" He said to him, "You have said so."

26   Now as they were eating, Jesus took bread, and blessed, and broke it, and gave it to the disciples and said, "Take, eat; this is my body."

27   And he took a cup, and when he had given thanks he gave it to them, saying, "Drink of it, all of you;

28   for this is my blood of the covenant, which is poured out for many for the forgiveness of sins.

29   I tell you I shall not drink again of this fruit of the vine until that day when I drink it new with you in my Father's kingdom."

Mark 14:12-25

12   And on the first day of Unleavened Bread, when they sacrificed the passover lamb, his disciples said to him, "Where will you have us go and prepare for you to eat the passover?"

13   And he sent two of his disciples, and said to them, "Go into the city, and a man carrying a jar of water will meet you; follow him,

14   and wherever he enters, say to the householder, 'The Teacher says, Where is my guest room, where I am to eat the passover with my disciples?'

15   And he will show you a large upper room furnished and ready; there prepare for us."

16   And the disciples set out and went to the city, and found it as he had told them; and they prepared the passover.

17   And when it was evening he came with the twelve.

18   And as they were at table eating, Jesus said, "Truly I say to you, one of you will betray me, one who is eating with me."

19   They began to be sorrowful, and to say to him one after another, "Is it I?"

20   He said to them, "It is one of the twelve, one who is dipping bread in the same dish with me.

21   For the Son of man goes as it is written of him, but woe to that man by whom the Son of man is betrayed! It would have been better for that man if he had not been born."

22   And as they were eating, he took bread, and blessed, and broke it, and gave it to them, and said, "Take; this is my body."

23   And he took a cup, and when he had given thanks he gave it to them, and they all drank of it.

24   And he said to them, "This is my blood of the covenant, which is poured out for many.

25   Truly, I say to you, I shall not drink again of the fruit of the vine until that day when I drink it new in the kingdom of God."

Luke 22:7-20

7   They came the day of Unleavened Bread, on which the passover lamb had to be sacrificed.

8   So Jesus sent Peter and John, saying, "Go and prepare the passover for us, that we may eat it."

9   They said to him, "Where will you have us prepare it."

10 He said to them, "Behold, when you have entered the city, a man carrying a jar of water will meet you; follow him into the house which he enters,

11	and tell the householder, 'The teacher says to you, Where is the guest room, where I am to eat the passover with my disciples?'
12	And he will show you a large upper room furnished; there make ready."
13	And they went, and found it as he had told them; and they prepared the passover.
14	And when the hour came, he sat at table, and the apostles with him.
15	And he said to them, "I have earnestly desired to eat this passover with you before I suffer;
16	for I tell you I shall not eat it until it is fulfilled in the kingdom of God."
17	And he took a cup, and when he had given thanks he said, "Take this, and divide it among yourselves;
18	for I tell you that from now on I shall not drink of the fruit of the vine until the kingdom of God comes."
19	And he took bread, and when he had given thanks he broke it and gave it to them saying, "This is my body."
20	And likewise the cup after supper, saying, "This cup which is poured out for you is the new covenant in my blood."

---

[1] The Holy Bible, Revised Standard Version, New York: Thomas Nelson and Sons, 1952, 781; 800; 830.

FOOTNOTES

1   Cecil Roth, *The Historical Background of the Dead Sea Scrolls*, New York: Philosophical Library, Inc., 1959, 23-52.

2   Geoffrey Driver, *The Judaean Scrolls*, New York: Schocken Books, Inc., 1965, 266-284.

3   Louis Finkelstein, ed., *The Jews, Their History, Culture and Religion*, 2 vols., New York: Harper and Brothers, 1960, 1, 136-140.

4   D. S. Russell, *Between the Testaments*, Philadelphia: Fortress Press, 1965, 54.

5   John Bright, *A History of Israel*, Philadelphia: The Westminster Press, MCMLIX, 450.

6   John E. Pryke, "Beliefs and Practices of the Qumran Community," *The Church Quarterly Review*, July-September, 1967, 168:318.

7   Millar Burrows, *The Dead Sea Scrolls*, New York: The Viking Press, 1955, 172.

8   W. D. Davies, *Introduction to Pharisaism*, Philadelphia: Fortress Press, 1967, 17-24.

9   William H. Brownlee, *The Meaning of the Qumran Scrolls for the Bible*, New York: Oxford University Press, 1964, 58-59.

10 Edmund Sutcliffe, *The Monks of Qumran*, Maryland: The Newman Press, 1960, 16-18.

11 Frank Moore Cross, Jr., *The Ancient Library of Qumran and Modern Biblical Studies*, Revised Edition, Garden City, New York: Doubleday and Company, Inc., 1961, 53-54.

12 Jozef T. Milik, *Ten Years of Discovery in the Wilderness of Judea*, Studies in Biblical Theology, No. 26, J. Strugnell, trans., London: SCM Press Ltd., 1959, 11.

13 Lockwood and Son, 1913, 303-304.

14   Ludwig Koehler and Walter Baumgartner, eds., <u>Lexicon in Veteris Testamenti Libros</u>, Leiden, Netherlands: E. J. Brill, 1953, 495.

15   C. C. McCown, "The Scene of John's Ministry and Its Relation to the Purpose and Outcome of his Mission," <u>Journal of Biblical Literature</u>, LIX, 113.

16   Robert Funk, "The Wilderness," <u>Journal of Biblical Literature,</u> 1959, 78, 205-214.

17   Milik, 50-54; Stauffer, <u>Jesus and the Wilderness Community at Qumran,</u> 1-2.

18   J. Van Der Ploeg, <u>The Excavations at Qumran</u>, Kevin Smyth, trans., New York: Longmans, Green and Co., 1958, 62-68.

19.   Roth, <u>The Historical Background of the Dead Sea Scrolls</u>, 3-6.

20   Finkelstein, ed., <u>The Jews, Their History, Culture and Religion</u>, I, 134-135.

21   Burrows, <u>The Dead Sea Scrolls</u>, 245.

22   J. Lindblom, <u>Prophecy in Ancient Israel</u>, Philadelphia: Fortress Press, 1967, 360.

23   George F. Moore, <u>Judaism</u>, 3 vols., Cambridge, Mass.: Harvard University Press, 1962, 2, 378.

24   Lindblom, <u>Prophecy in Ancient Israel</u>, 360-363.

25   Moore, <u>Judaism</u>, 2, 378.

26   <u>Ibid</u>., 378-379.

27   Ringgren, 166; LaSor, 93; Schubert, 98-99; Burrows, <u>The Dead Sea Scrolls,</u> 271-272.

28   Kurt Schubert, <u>The Dead Sea Community: Its Origin and Teachings,</u> London: Adam and Charles Black Ltd., 1959, 98-99.

29   William LaSor, *The Dead Sea Scrolls and The New Testament,* Michigan: William Eerdmans Publishing Co., 1972, 105.

30   *Ibid.*, 100.

31   Charles Pfeiffer, *The Dead Sea Scrolls and The Bible*, Grand Rapids, Michigan: Baker Book House, 1969.

32   LaSor, 105; Schubert, 111.

33   W. O. Oesterley and Theodore Robinson, *Hebrew Religion*, New York: The MacMillan Co., 1930, 353.

34   LaSor, 103.

35   Oesterley and Robinson, 356.

36   John L. McKenzie, *Dictionary of the Bible,* Milwaukee: The Bruce Publishing Co., 1965, 569-571.

37   Moore, 2, 374, 376.

38   LaSor, 104; Burrows, *The Dead Sea Scrolls,* 272.

39   LaSor, 105; Kevin Smyth, *The Dead Sea Scrolls*, London: Catholic Truth Society, 1956, 19; Sutcliffe, *The Monks of Qumran,* 84-85.

40   Helmer Ringgren, *The Faith of Qumran*, Emilie T. Sander, trans., Philadelphia, Pennsylvania: Fortress Press, 1963, 167.

41   Sutcliffe, *The Monks of Qumran,* 84.

42   LaSor, 102.

43   Brownlee, *The Meaning of the Qumran Scrolls for the Bible*, 98-99.

44   Pfeiffer, 130.

45   Karl Kuhn, "The Two Messiahs of Aaron and Israel," in Krister Stendahl, ed., *The Scrolls and the New Testament*, New York: Harper and Brothers, 1957, 60.

46   Milik, 124-126.

47   Burrows, The Dead Sea Scrolls, 272.

48   Ringgren, 169.

49   Sutcliffe, The Monks of Qumran, 84-85.

50   LaSor, 105.

51   Cecil Roth and Geoffrey Wigoders, eds., Encyclopedia Judaica, 16 vols., New York: The Maxillan Company, 11, 1409.

52   Ibid., 1410.

53   A. Van den Born, Encyclopedic Dictionary of the Bible, Louis Hartman, trans., New York: McGraw-Hill Book Company, Inc., 1963, 1523.

54   Sutcliffe, The Monks of Qumran, 86-87.

55   John M. Allegro, The Dead Sea Scrolls and the Origins of Christianity, New York: Criterion Books, 1967, 96-98.

56   Kevin Smyth, The Dead Sea Scrolls, London: Catholic Truth Society, 1956, 17.

57   Brownlee, The Meaning of the Qumran Scrolls for the Bible, 128.

58   Cecil Roth, The Dead Sea Scrolls, A New Historical Approach, New York: W. W. Norton and Co., Inc., 1965, VIII.

59   Burrows, The Dead Sea Scrolls, 334.

60   Vermes, Discovery in the Judean Desert, 67.

61   Cross, Jr., 101.

62   Ringgren, 198.

63   Isidore Singer, ed., The Jewish Encyclopeida, 12 vols., New York: KTAV Publishing House, Inc., 1901, 8, 511; Van den Born, 1523.

64   Roth and Wigoder, ed., II, 1411.

65   Singer, ed., 8, 512.

66   Burrows, The Dead Sea Scrolls, 19.

67   Ibid., 223.

68   Ibid., 25. Van Der Ploeg, The Excavations at Qumran, 170.

69   Milik, 37.

70   A. Dupont-Sommer, The Jewish Sect of Qumran and the Essenes, R. Barnett, trans., New York: The MacMillan Company, 1956, 59.

71   Vermes, The Dead Sea Scrolls in English, 118.

72   Schubert, 7.

73   Sutcliffe, The Monks of Qumran, 97.

74   De Vaux, Archaeology and the Dead Sea Scrolls, 12-14.

75   Schubert, 53.

76   R. K. Harrison, "The Rites and Customs and the Qumran Sect," in Matthew Black, ed., The Scrolls and Christianity, Theological Collections II, London: The Talbot Press, 1969, 33.

77   Allegro, 131-132.

78   Cross, Jr., 69-70.

79   Sutcliffe, The Monks of Qumran, 83.

80   J. Van Der Ploeg, "The Meals of the Essenes," Journal of Semitic Studies, April, 1957, 2, 173.

81.   Vermes, The Dead Sea Scrolls in English, 49.

82   Ibid.

83   Ibid., 49.

84   Pfeiffer, 56.

85   Smyth, 22.

86   LaSor, 68, 102.

87   Dupont-Sommer, 99.

88   Ringgren, 219, 245.

89   John E. Groh, "The Qumran Meal and the Last Supper," Concordia Quarterly Monthly, May, 1970, 41, 286.

90   Vermes, Discovery in the Judean Desert, 39, 55.

91   Milik, 106.

92   Allegro, 131-132.

93   Pryke, "The Sacraments of Holy Baptism and Holy Communion in the Light of the Ritual Washings and Sacred Meals at Qumran," 5, 547.

94   Brown, Fitzmyer, and Murphy, eds., Section 68, 93-96, 553-554. A person, place or thing may be sacred in the sense that they have been blessed or consecrated for use in the service of God.

95   Geoffrey Driver, The Judean Scrolls, New York: Schocken Books, Inc., 1965, 506-513.

96   Rowley, "Qumran Sect and Christian Origins," Bulletin of the John Ryland's Library, 1961-1962, XLIV, 144-145.

97   Yigael Yadin, The Message of the Scrolls; New York: The University Press, 1962, 120-121.

98   C. S. Mann, "The Scrolls, the Lord and the Primitive Church," The Church Quarterly Review, October-December, 1958, 159, 522.

99   Van Der Ploeg, "The Meals of the Essenes," 171; Van Der Ploeg, The Excavations at Qumran, 213.

100   Sutcliffe, "Sacred Meals at Qumran?" 51-52.

101   Schubert, 53.

102   Millar Burrows, More Light on the Dead Sea Scrolls, New York: The Viking Press, 1958, 369-370.

103   McKenzie, Dictionary of the Bible, 715.

104   Cross, Jr., 234.

105   Edward Kilmartin, The Eucharist in the Primitive Church, Englewood Cliffs, New Jersey: Prentice-Hall, Inc., 1965, 9.

106   Vermes, The Dead Sea Scrolls in English, 47.

107   A. Powell Davies, The Meaning of the Dead Sea Scrolls, New York: The New American Library, 1956, 98-99.

108   Edmund Wilson, The Dead Sea Scrolls 1947-1969, New York: Oxford.

109   John Priest, "The Messiah and the Meal in IQSa," Journal of Biblical Literature, March, 1963, 82-97.

110   Bruce, The New Testament History, 103-104.

111   De Vaux, Archaeology and the Dead Sea Scrolls, iii.

112   Karlheinz Muller, "Qumran," in K. Rahner, C. Ernst, and K. Smyth, eds., Sacramentum Mundi, An Encyclopedia of Theology, 6 vols., New York: Herder and Herder, 1970, 5, 177.

113   Louis Boyer, Eucharist, Charles U. Quinn, trans., Notre Dame: University of Notre Dame Press, 1968, 49.

114   Karl Kuhn, "The Lord's Supper and the Communal Meal at Qumran," in Krister Stendahl, ed., Scrolls and the New Testament, New York: Harper and Brothers, 1957, 77.

115   Charles Fritsch, The Qumran Community, New York: The MacMillan Company, 1956, 123.

116   Pfeiffer, 56.

117   Harrison, "The Rites and Customs of the Qumran Sect," in Black, ed., 32-33.

118   P. Parente, A. Piolanti, and S. Garofalo, eds., Dictionary of Dogmatic Theology, E. Doronzo, trans., Wisconsin: The Bruce Publishing Company, 1957, 246.

119   Ibid., 246-247.

120   Brown, "The Dead Sea Scrolls and the New Testament," in Charlesworth, ed., 4.

121   Black, The Scrolls and Christian Origins, 104-105.

122   Von Allemn, ed., 41.

123   Steinmueller and Sullivan, eds., Section 2, 85.

124   J. M'Clintock and J. Strong, eds., Cyclopaedia of Biblical Theological and Ecclesiastical Literature, X. vols., New York: Arno Press, 1969, V. 514.

125   Clifton J. Allen, ed., The Broadman Bible Commentary: General Articles Luke-John, 12 vols., Nashville, Tennessee: Broadman Press, 1969, 9, 384.

126   James Hastings, ed., Dictionary of the Bible, Frederick Grant and H. H. Rowley, eds., Revised Edition, New York: Charles Scribner's Sons, 1963, 274.

127   Jeremias, The Eucharistic Words of Jesus, 63.

128   M. H. Sheperd, Jr., "The Lord's Supper," The Interpreter's Dictionary of the Bible, 4 vols., George A. Buttricm, ed., New York: Abingdon Press, 1962, 3, 73.

129   Hayim H. Donin, To Be a Jew, New York: Basic Books, Inc., Publishers, 1972, 221.

130   J. Delorme, "The Last Supper and the Pasch in the New Testament," in J. Delorme, P. Benoit, J. Dupont, M. E. Boismard, and D. Mallat, The Eucharist in the New Testament, E. M. Stewart, trans., Baltimore, Maryland: Helicon Press, 1964, 31.

131   Roth and Wigoder, eds., 1972, 4, 1334. James Hastings, ed., *A Dictionary of the Bible*, New York: Charles Scribner's Sons, 1903, 1, 151.

132   Delorme, "The Last Supper and the Pasch in the New Testament," in Delorme, *et al.*, 22-24.

133   Jeremias, *The Eucharistic Words of Jesus*, 27.

134   Hans Conzelmann, *An Outline of the Theology of the New Testament*, John Bowden, trans., New York: Harper and Row, Publishers, 1969, 52.

135   Kuhn, "The Lord's Supper and the Communal Meal at Qumran," in Stendahl, ed., *The Scrolls and the New Testament*, 81.

136   G. Kittel and G. Bromiley, eds., *Theological Dictionary of the New Testament*, 9 vols., G. Bromiley, trans., Grand Rapids, Michigan: William B. Eerdmans Publishing Company, 1965, 3, 728-729.

137   A. J. B. Higgins, *The Lord's Supper in the New Testament*, London: SCM Press, Ltd., 1964, 52.

138   Kittel and Bromiley, eds., 3, 736.

139   Von Allmen, ed., 41.

140   Eduard Schweizer, *The Lord's Supper According to the New Testament*, James Davies, trans., Philadelphia: Fortress Press, 1967, 26.

141   M'Clintock and Strong, eds., V, 514.

142   Groh, "The Qumran Meal and the Last Supper," 289; Shepherd, Jr., "The Lord's Supper," 159.

143   Zeitlin, "The Dead Sea Scrolls: A Travesty on Scholarship," 9.

144   Beyer, 2, 760-761.

145   Roth and Wigoder, eds., 7, 838.

146   Donin, 233.

147   Driver, 515.

148   Rowley, The Dead Sea Scrolls and the New Testament, 16.

149   Hugh Anderson, Jesus and Christian Origins, New York: Oxford University Press, 1964, 294-297.

150   Edmund Wilson, The Dead Sea Scrolls 1947-1969, New York: Oxford.

151   Yngve Brilioth, Eucharistic Faith and Practice, Evangelical and Catholic, A. G. Herbert, trans., New York: The MacMillan Co., 1939.

152   Ibid., 10, 38-39.

153   G. H. Box, "The Jewish Antecedents of the Eucharist," Journal of Theological Studies, 1902, III, 368.

154   Driver, 511.

155   Box, 360-361.

156   Edward Kilmartin, The Eucharist in the Primitive Church, Englewood Cliffs, New Jersey: Prentice-Hall, Inc., 1965, 10.

157   Joseph Klausner, From Jesus to Paul, William F. Stinespring, trans., Boston: Beacon Press, 1961, 258.

158   Klausner, 277.

159   Black, The Scroll and Christian Origins, 115.

160   Solomon Zeitlin, The Rise and Fall of the Judaean State, 2 vols., Philadelphia, Pennsylvania: The Jewish Publication Society of American, 1962, 1, 201.

161   M. H. Shepherd, Jr., "Haburot," The Interpreter's Bible, 12 vols., George Buttrick, ed., New York: Abingdon Press, 1951, 3, 74.

162   Jack Finegan, <u>Light from the Ancient Past</u>, Princeton, New Jersey: Princeton University Press, 1959, 290.

163   McKenzie, <u>Dictionary of the Bible</u>, 558-559.

164   C. H. Dobb, <u>The Apostolic Preaching</u>, New York: Harper and Row, Publishers, 1964, 93.

165   Willi Marxsen, <u>The Beginnings of Christology: A Study in Its Problems</u>, Paul Achtemeier, trans., Philadelphia, Pennsylvania: Fortress Press, 1969, 63.

166   Clifton J. Allen, ed., <u>The Broadman Bible Commentary: General Articles Matthew-Mark</u>, Nashville, Tennessee: Broadman Press, 1969, 8, 233-234.

167   A. Powell Davies, <u>The Meaning of the Dead Sea Scrolls</u>, 99.

168   Johannes Betz, "Eucharist," <u>Sacramentum Mundi, An Encyclopedia of Theology</u>, 6 vols., Karl Rahner, Cornelius Ernst, and Devin Smyth, eds., New York: Herder and Herder, 1970, 2, 257-258.

169   Schweizer, 3, 24.

170   Walter Bundy, <u>Jesus and the First Three Gospels</u>, Cambridge, Massachusetts: Harvard University Press, 1955, 488-494.

171   Delorme, "The Last Supper and the Pasch in the New Testament," in Delorme, <u>et al.</u>, 40.

172   James Kallas, <u>Jesus and the Power of Satan</u>, Philadelphia, Pennsylvania: The Westminster Press, MCMLXVIII, 182.

173   Jeremias, <u>The Eucharistic Words of Jesus</u>, 84.

174   Harrison, <u>The Dead Sea Scrolls</u>, 124.

175   A. J. B. Higgins, <u>The Lord's Supper in the New Testament</u>, 22-23.

176   Anderson, *Jesus and Christian Origins*, 291.

177   W. F. Albright and C. S. Mann, *The Gospel According to Matthew, The Anchor Bible,* Garden City, New York: Doubleday and Company, Inc., 1966, 320.

178   Oscar Cullmann and F. L. Leenhardt, *Essays on the Lord's Supper,* J. G. Davies, trans., Richmond, Virginia: John Knox Press, 1968, 39.

179   Eugene Ruchstuhl, *Chronology of the Last Days of Jesus,* Victor Drapela, trans., New York: Desclee Co., 1965, 24-27.

180   Johannes Behm, "The Last Supper," *Theological Dictionary of the New Testament,* 9 vols., G. Kittel and G. Bromiley, eds., G. Bromiley, trans., Grand Rapids, Michigan: William B. Eerdmans Publishing Company, 1965, 3, 732-734.

181   Benoit, "The Accounts of the Institution and What They Imply," in Delorme, et al., 73-86.

182   F. F. Bruce, *The New Testament History*, London: Thomas Nelson and Sons, Ltd., 1969, 101-104; Millar Burrows, *The Dead Sea Scrolls*, New York: The Viking Press, 1955, 240.

183   Danielou, *The Dead Sea Scrolls and Primitive Christianity*, 27.

184   Stauffer, *Jesus and the Wilderness Community at Qumran,* 16.

185   Edmund Sutcliffe, *The Monks of Qumran*, Westminster, Maryland: The Newman Press, 1960, 112-113, 123.

186   Clifton Allen, ed., 9, 165.

187   Van den Borg, 299-300.

188   Roth and Widoder, eds., 5, 52.

189   *Ibid.,* 54.

190   Schubert, *The Dead Sea Community: Its Origin and Teachings*, 142.

191 Max Thurian, The Eucharistic Memorial, 2 vols., J. G. Davies, trans., Richmond, Virginia: John Knox Press, 1968, 1, 87.

192 Shepherd, J., "The Lord's Supper," The Interpreter's Dictionary of the Bible, 3, 74-75.

193 G. D. Kilpatrick, "Living Issues in Biblical Scholarship, The Last Supper," The Expository Times, Oct., 1952, 64:1:4-8.

194 Van den Borg, 1306; Shepherd, Jr., "The Lord's Supper," 3, 74-75.

195 Von Allmen, ed., 239-240; M. H. Shepher, Jr., The Pascal Liturgy and the Apocalypse, Richmond Virginia: John Knox Press, 1960, 14.

196 Pierre Benoit, "Qumran and the New Testament," in Jerome Murphy-O'Connor, ed., Paul and Qumran, Chicago, Illinois: The Priory Press, 1968, 9.

197 Davies, The Meaning of the Dead Sea Scrolls, 99-100.

198 Martin A. Larson, The Essene Heritage, New York: Philosophical Library, 1967, 170.

199 Allegro, The Dead Sea Scrolls and the Origins of Christianity, 160.

200 Geza Vermes, Discovery in the Judean Desert, New York: Desclee Company, 1956, 47.

201 Allegro, 164-165.

202 McKenzie, Dictionary of the Bible, 251.

203 Milik, Ten Years of Discovery in the Wilderness of Judaea, 106.

204 H. H. Rowley, "The Qumran Sect and Christian Origins," Bulletin of the John Ryland's Library, 1961-62, XLIV, 143.

205 Solomon Zeitlin, "The Dead Sea Scrolls: A Travesty on Scholarship," Jewish Quarterly Review, 1956-57, XLVII, 10.

206   Joachim Heremias, *The Eucharistic Words of Jesus*, Norman Perrin, trans., New York: Charles Scribner's Sons, 1966, 35-36.

207   Burrows, *More Light on the Dead Sea Scrolls*, 82.

208   Smyth, *The Dead Sea Scrolls*, 23.

209   Driver, 513.

210   John E. Groh, "The Qumran Meal and the Last Supper," *Concordia Quarterly Monthly*, May, 1970, 41, 294.

211   Karl Kuhn, "The Lord's Supper and the Communal Meal at Qumran," in Krister Stendahl, ed., *The Scrolls and the New Testament*, New York: Harper and Brothers, 1957, 84-85.

212   Matthew Black, *The Scrolls and Christian Origins*, New York: Charles Scribner's Sons, 1961, 168.

213   R. K. Harrison, *The Dead Sea Scrolls*, New York: Harper and Row Publishers, 1961, 117-124.

214   Ringgren, *The Faith of Qumran*, 245.

215   F. F. Bruce, "Jesus and the Gospels in the Light of the Scrolls," in Matthew Black, ed., *The Scrolls and Christianity*, London: The Talbot Press, 1969, 77-78.

216   Cyrus Gordon, *Adventures in the Nearest East*, London: Phoenix House Ltd., 1957, 141.

217   Ethelbert Stauffer, *Jesus and the Wilderness Community at Qumran*, Hans Spalteholz, trans., Philadelphia, Pennsylvania: Fortress Press, 1964, 5.

218   Jean Danielou, *The Dead Sea Scrolls and Primitive Christianity*, Salvator Attanasio, trans., Baltimore, Maryland: Helicon Press, Inc., 1958, 29.

219   Raymond E. Brown, "The Dead Sea Scrolls and the New Testament," in James Charlesworth, ed., *John and Qumran*, London: Geoffrey Chapman, 1972, 34.

220   LaSor, *The Dead Sea Scrolls and the New Testament*, 165.

221   Jean Carmignac, <u>Christ and the Teacher of Righteousness,</u> Katherine G. Pedley, trans., Baltimore, Maryland: Helicon Press, 1962, 94.

222   H. H. Rowley, <u>The Dead Sea Scrolls and the New Testament,</u> London: The Talbot Press, 1964, 17.

223   A. G. M. P. Higgins, "A Few Thoughts on the Dead Sea Scrolls," <u>Modern Churchmen</u>, January, 1970, 13, 199.

224   J. L. Teicher, "Jesus' Sayings in the Dead Sea Scrolls," <u>Journal of Jewish Studies</u>, 1954, 6, 38.

225   Borge Hjerl-Hansen, "Did Christ Know the Qumran Sect?" <u>Revue de Qumran,</u> July 1958-July 1959, I, 500.

226   Burrows, <u>More Light on the Dead Sea Scrolls,</u> 93.

BIBLIOGRAPHY

BOOKS

Albright, William F. *The Archaeology of Palestine.* Baltimore, Maryland: Penguin Books, 1954.

Albright, William F. *From the Stone Age to Christianity.* Garden City, New York: Doubleday and Company, Inc., 1957.

Allegro, John M. *The Dead Sea Scrolls and the Origins of Christianity.* New York: Criterion Books, 1967.

Allen, Clifton J., ed., *The Broadman Bible Commentary: General Articles Luke-John.* 12 vols. Nashville, Tennessee: Broadman Press, 1969.

Allen, Clifton J., ed., *The Broadman Bible Commentary: General Articles Matthew-Mark.* 12 vols. Nashville, Tennessee: Broadman Press, 1969.

Allen, W. "Matthew," *A Dictionary of Christ and the Gospels.* 2 vols. James Hastings, ed., New York: Charles Scribner's Sons, 1908, 2, 146-148.

Anderson, Hugh. *Jesus and Christian Origins.* New York: Oxford University Press, 1964.

Baron, Salo and Blau, Joseph. *Judaism.* New York: The Bobbs-Merrill Company, Inc., 1954.

Behm, Johannes. "The Last Supper," *Theological Dictionary of the New Testament.* 9 vols. G. Kittel and G. Bromiley, eds., G. Bromiley, trans., Grand Rapids, Michigan: William B. Eerdmans Publishing Company, 1965, 3, 732-743.

Betz, Johannes. "Eucharist," *Sacramentum Mundi: An Encyclopedia of Theology.* 6 vols. Karl Rahner, Cornelius Ernst, and Kevin Smyth eds. New York: Herder and Herder, 1970, 2, 257-266.

Black, Matthew. *The Scrolls and Christian Origins.* New York: Charles Scribner's Sons, 1961.

Black, Matthew, ed. *The Scrolls and Christianity*. Theological Collections II. London: The Talbot Press, 1969.

Bouyer, Louis. *Eucharist*. Charles U. Quinn, trans. Notre Dame: University of Notre Dame Press, 1968.

Bright, John. *A History of Israel*. Philadelphia, Pennsylvania: The Westminster Press, 1959.

Brilioth, Ynyve. *Eucharistic Faith and Practices, Evangelical and Catholic*. A. G. Herbert, trans. New York: The MacMillan Company, 1939.

Brown, Raymond E. "The Dead Sea Scrolls and the New Testament," in James H. Charlesworth, ed. *John and Qumran*. London: Geoffrey Chapman, 1972, 1-8.

Brown, Raymond E., Fitzmyer, James A., and Murphy, Roland E., eds., *The Jerome Biblical Commentary*. Englewood Cliffs, New Jersey: Prentice-Hall, Inc., 1968.

Brownlee, William H. "The Dead Sea Manual of Discipline: Translation and Notes," *Bulletin of the American Schools of Oriental Research*, Supplementary Studies Nos. 10-12. New Haven, Connecticut: American Schools of Oriental Research, 1951, 11-30.

Brownlee, William H. *The Meaning of the Qumran Scrolls for the Bible*. New York: Oxford University Press, 1964.

Bruce, F. F. *The New Testament History*. London: Thomas Nelson and Sons Ltd., 1969.

Burrows, Millar. *The Dead Sea Scrolls*. New York: The Viking Press, 1955.

Burrows, Millar. *More Light on the Dead Sea Scrolls*. New York: The Viking Press, 1958.

Buttrick, George, ed. *The Interpreter's Bible*. 12 vols. New York: Abingdon Press, 1951.

Carmignac, Jean. *Christ and the Teacher of Righteousness*. Katherine G. Pedley, trans. Beltimore, Maryland: Helicon Press, 1962.

Charlesworth, James H., ed. *John and Qumran*. London: Geoffrey Chapman, 1972.

Cross, Jr., Frank Moore. *The Ancient Library of Qumran and Modern and Biblical Studies*. Revised Edition. Garden City, New York: Doubleday and Company, Inc., 1961.

Cullmann, Oscar and Leenhardt, F. L. *Essays on the Lord's Supper.* J. G. Davies, trans. Richmond, Virginia: John Knox Press, 1968.

Danielou, Jean. *The Dead Sea Scrolls and Primitive Christianity.* Salvator Attanasio trans. Baltimore, Maryland: Helicon Press Inc., 1958.

Davies, A. Powell. *The Meaning of the Dead Sea Scrolls.* New York: The New American Library, 1956.

Davies, W. D. *Introduction to Pharaism.* Philadelphia, Pennsylvania: Fortress Press, 1967.

Davies, W. D. *Invitation to the New Testament*. Garden City, New York: Doubleday and Company, Inc., 1966.

De Vaux, Roland. *Ancient Israel*. 2 vols. John McHugh trans. New York: McGraw-Hill Book Company, Inc., 1961.

De Vaux, Roland. *Archaeology and the Dead Sea Scrolls.* London: Oxford University Press, 1973.

Donin, Hayim H. *To Be A Jew*. New York: Basic Books, Inc., 1972.

Driver, Geoffrey. *The Judean Scrolls*. New York: Schocken Books, Inc., 1965.

Dupont-Sommer, A. *The Jewish Sect of Qumran and the Essenes*. R. D. Barnett trans. New York: The MacMillan Company, 1956.

Finegan, Jack. *Light from the Ancient Past*. Princeton, New Jersey: Princeton University Press, 1959.

Finkelstein, Louis, ed. *The Jews, Their Culture and Religion.* 2 vols. New York: Harper and Brothers, 1960.

Flusser, David. "The Dead Sea Sect and the Pre-Pauline Christianity," *Scripta Hierosolymitana.* 4 vols. C. Rabin and Y. Yadin eds., Jerusalem: The Magna Press, 1958, 4, 215-266.

Freedman, David and Greenfield, Jonas eds., *New Directions in Biblical Archaeology.* New York: Doubleday and Company, Inc., 1971.

Fritsch, Charles T. *The Qumran Community.* New York: The MacMillan Company, 1956.

Gordon, Cyrus H. *Adventures in the Nearest East.* London: Phoenix House Ltd., 1957.

Harrison, R. K. *The Dead Sea Scrolls.* New York: Harper and Row Publishers, 1961.

Hastings, James, ed. *A Dictionary of the Bible.* Revised Edition. Frederick Grant and H. H. Rowley, eds., New York: Charles Scribner's Sons, 1963.

Higgins, A. J. B. *The Lord's Supper in the New Testament.* London: SCM Press Ltd., 1964.

Jeremias, Joachim. *The Eucharistic Words of Jesus.* Arnold Ehrhardt, trans. New York: Charles Scribner's Sons, 1966.

Jeremias, Joachim. *New Testament Theology.* John Bowden, trans. New York: Charles Scribner's Sons, 1971.

Kilmartin, Edward J. *The Eucharist in the Primitive Church.* Englewood Cliffs, New Jersey: Prentice-Hall, 1965.

Kittel, G. and Bromiley G., eds., *Theological Dictionary of the New Testament.* 9 vols. G. Bromiley, trans. Grand Rapids, Michigan: William B. Eerdmans Publishing Company, 1965.

Klausner, Joseph. *From Jesus to Paul.* William F. Steinespring, trans. Boston: Beacon Press, 1961.

Kummel, Werner. *Introduction to the New Testament.* A. J. Mattill, Jr., trans. Nashville, Tennessee: Abingdon Press, 1966.

Landman, Isaac, ed. *The Universal Jewish Encyclopedia.*
    10 vols. New York: KTAV Publishing House, Inc., 1969.

Landman, Isaac, ed. "Wilderness," *The Universal Jewish Encyclopedia.* 10 vols. New York: KTAV Publishing House, Inc., 1969, 10, 519-521.

LaSor, William. *The Dead Sea Scrolls and the New Testament.*
    Grand Rapids, Michigan: William B. Eerdmans Publishing Company, 1972.

Leaney, A. R. C. *The Rule of Qumran and Its Meaning.*
    Philadelphia, Pennsylvania: The Westminster Press, 1966.

Leon-DuFour, Xavier. *Dictionary of Biblical Theology.*
    P. J. Cahill, trans. New York: Desclee Company Inc., 1967.

Leon-DuFour, Xavier. *The Gospels and the Jesus of History.*
    John McHugh, trans. and ed. New York: Image Books, 1970.

Lindblom, J. *Prophecy in Ancient Israel.* Philadelphia, Pennsylvania: Fortress Press, 1967.

Marxsen, Willi. *The Beginnings of Christology: A Study in Its Problems.* Paul J. Achtemeier, trans. Philadelphia, Pennsylvania: Fortress Press, 1969.

M'Clintock, J. and Strong, J., eds. *Cyclopaedia of Biblical, Theological and Ecclesiastical Literature.* 10 vols.
    New York: Arno Press, 1969.

M'Clintock, J. and Strong, J., eds. "Lustrations," *Cyclopaedia of Biblical, Theological and Ecclesiastical Literature,* 10 vols, New York: Arno Press, 1969, V, 563-564.

M'Clintock, J. and Strong, J. "Rite," *Cyclopaedia of Biblical, Theological and Ecclesiastical Literature.* X. vols.
    New York: Arno Press, 1969, IX, 514-515.

McKenzie, John L. *Dictionary of the Bible.* Milwaukee, Wisconsin: The Bruce Publishing Company, 1965.

Milik, Josef T. Ten Years of Discovery in the Wilderness of
    Judea. Studies in Biblical Theology No. 26. J. Strugnell,
    trans. Naperville, Illinois: Alec R. Allenson Inc.,
    1959.

Moore, George Moore. Judaism. 3 vols. Cambridge, Massachusetts:
    Harvard University Press, 1962.

Montefiore, G. G. and Loewe, H., eds. A Rabbinic Anthology.
    London: The MacMillan Company Ltd., 1938.

Muller, Karlheinz. "Qumran," Sacramentum Mundi, An Encyclopedia
    of Theology. K. Rayner, E. Ernst, and K. Smyth, eds.
    6 vols. New York: Herder and Herder, 1970, 5, 177-178.

Murphy, Roland E. The Dead Sea Scrolls and the Bible.
    Westminster, Maryland: The Newman Press, 1957.

Oesterley, W. O. and Robinson, Theodore. Hebrew Religion.
    New York: The MacMillan Company, 1930.

Parente, P., Piolanti, A., and Garofalo, S. Dictionary of
    Dogmatic Theology. E. Doronzo, trans. Milwaukee,
    Wisconsin: The Bruce Publishing Company, 1957.

Pfeiffer, Charles F. The Dead Sea Scrolls and the Bible.
    Grand Rapids, Michigan: Baker Book House, 1969.

Rabin, Chaim. Qumran Studies. London: Oxford University Press,
    1957.

Rae, Frederick. "Mark," in James Hastings, ed. A Dictionary
    of Christ and the Gospels. 2 vols. New York: Charles
    Scribner and Sons, 1908, 2, 119-120.

Rahner, Karl, Ernst, Cornelius, and Smyth, Kevin, eds.
    Sacramentum Mundi, An Encyclopedia of Theology. 6 vols.
    New York: Herder and Herder, 1970.

Rengstorf, Karl H. Hirbet Qumran and the Problem of the
    Library of the Dead Sea Caves. Leiden, Netherlands:
    E. J. Brill, 1963.

Ringgren, Helmer. The Faith of Qumran. Emilie T. Sander,
    trans. Philadelphia, Pennsylvania: Fortress Press,
    1963.

Roth, Cecil. *The Dead Sea Scrolls, A New Historical Approach*.
New York: W. W. Norton and Company, Inc., 1965.

Roth, Cecil. *The Historical Background of the Dead Sea Scrolls*.
New York: Philosophical Library Inc., 1959.

Roth, Cecil and Wigoder, Geoffrey, eds. *Encyclopedia Judaica*.
16 vols. New York: The MacMillan Company, 1972.

Roth, Cecil and Wigoder, Geoffrey, eds. "Wilderness,"
Encyclopedia Judaica. 16 vols. New York: The MacMillan Company, 1972, 16, 512-514.

Rowley, H. H. *The Dead Sea Scrolls and the New Testament*.
London: The Talbot Press, 1964.

Ruchstuhl, Eugene. *Chronology of the Last Days of Jesus*.
Victor Drapela, trans. New York: Desclee Company, 1965.

Sacher, Abram L. *A History of the Jews.* New York: Alfred A.
Knopf Inc., 1965.

Samuel, Athanasius Yeshue. *Treasure of Qumran*. London: Hodder and Stoughton, 1968.

Sanders, E. P. *The Tendencies of the Synoptic Tradition*.
Cambridge, England: Cambridge University Press, 1969.

Schubert, Kurt. *The Dead Sea Community: Its Origin and Teachings*.
London: Adam and Charles Black Ltd., 1959.

Schweizer, Eduard. *The Lord's Supper According to the New Testament.* James Davies, trans. Philadelphia, Pennsylvania: Fortress Press, 1967.

Selby, Donald J. *Introduction to the New Testament*. New York:
The MacMillan Company, 1971.

Shepherd, Jr., M. H. "Haburot," *The Interpreter's Bible.*
12 vols. George Buttrick, ed. New York: Abingdon Press, 1951, 3, 74-75.

Shepherd, Jr., M. H. "The Lord's Supper," *The Interpreter's Dictionary of the Bible*. 4 vols. George Buttrick, ed.
New York: Abingdon Press, 1962, 3, 73-75.

Shepherd, Jr., M. H. *The Pascal Liturgy and the Apocalypse.* Richmond, Virginia: John Knox Press, 1960.

Singer, Isidore, ed. *The Jewish Encyclopedia.* 12 vols. New York: KTAV Publishing House Inc., 1901.

Smyth, Kevin. *The Dead Sea Scrolls.* London: Catholic Truth Society, 1956.

Souter, Alex. "Luke," *A Dictionary of Christ and the Gospel.* 2 vols. New York: Charles Scribner and Sons, 1908, 2, 82-86.

Stagg, Frank. "Matthew," *The Broadman Bible Commentary: General Articles Matthew-Mark.* 12 vols. Nashville, Tennessee: Broadman Press, 1969, 8, 72-74.

Stauffer, Ethelbert. *Jesus and the Wilderness Community at Qumran.* Hans Spalteholz, trans. Philadelphia, Pennsylvania: Fortress Press, 1964.

Steinmueller, John and Sullivan, Kathryn, eds. *Catholic Biblical Encyclopedia Old and New Testament.* New York: Joseph F. Wagner Inc., 1956.

Stendahl, Krister. *The School of St. Matthew.* Philadelphia, Pennsylvania: Fortress Press, 1968.

Stendahl, Krister, ed. *The Scrolls and the New Testament.* New York: Harper and Brothers, 1957.

Sutcliffe, Edmund F. *The Monks of Qumran.* Westminster, Maryland: The Newman Press, 1960.

Taylor, Vincent. *The Gospels.* London: The Epworth Press, 1967.

Thurian, Max. *The Eucharistic Memorial.* 2 vols. J. G. Davies, trans. Richmond, Virginia: John Knox Press, 1968.

Tolbert, Malcolm. "Luke," *The Broadman Bible Commentary: General Articles Luke-John.* 12 vols. Nashville, Tennessee: Broadman Press, 1969, 9, 3-5.

Turlington, Henry. "Mark," *The Broadman Bible Commentary: General Articles Matthew-Mark.* 12 vols. Nashville, Tennessee: The Broadman Press, 1969, 8, 254-256.

Van den Born, A. *Encyclopedic Dictionary of the Bible.* Louis Hartmann, trans. New York: McGraw-Hill Book Company, Inc., 1963.

Van Der Ploeg, J. *The Excavations at Qumran.* Kevin Smyth, trans. New York: Longmans, Green and Company, 1958.

Vawter, Bruce. *The Four Gospels: An Introduction.* Garden City, New York: Doubleday and Company, 1967.

Vermes, Geza. *The Dead Sea Scrolls in English.* Baltimore, Maryland: Penguin Books, Inc., 1962.

Vermes, Geza. *Discovery in the Judean Desert.* New York: Desclee Company, 1956.

Von Allmen, J. J., ed. *A Company to the Bible.* New York: Oxford University Press, 1958.

Waxman, Meyer. *Judaism: Religion and Ethics.* New York: Thomas Yoseloff, 1958.

Wilson, C. W. "The Wilderness of Judaea," *A Dictionary of the Bible.* 4 vols. James Hastings, ed. New York: Charles Scribner's Sons, 1903, 2, 792-794.

Wilson, Edmund. *The Dead Sea Scrolls 1947-1969.* New York: Oxford University Press, 1969.

Wright, G. Ernest. *Biblical Archaeology.* Abridged Edition. Philadelphia, Pennsylvania: The Westminster Press, 1960.

Yadin, Yigael. *The Message of the Scrolls.* New York: The University Press, 1962.

Zeitlin, Solomon. *The Dead Sea Scrolls and Modern Scholarship.* Philadelphia, Pennsylvania: Dropsie College, 1956.

Zeitlin, Solomon. *The Rise and Fall of the Judaean State*.
    2 vols. Philadelphia, Pennsylvania: The Jewish
    Publication Society of American, 1962.

ESSAYS IN COLLECTIONS

Atkinson, Basil. "The Gospel According to Matthew," in
    Francis Davidson, ed. *The New Bible Commentary*.
    Grand Rapids, Michigan: William B. Eerdmans Publishing
    Company, 1965, 771-805.

Barr, Allen. "The Gospel According to Mark," in James
    Hastings, ed., Frederick Grant and H. H. Rowley, eds.,
    Revised Edition. *A Dictionary of the Bible*. New York:
    Charles Scribner's Sons, 1963, 622-624.

Benoit, P. "The Accounts of the Institution and What They
    Imply," in J. Delorme, P. Benoit, J. Dupont, M. E.
    Boismard, and D. Mollat. *The Eucharist in the New
    Testament*. Baltimore, Maryland: Helicon Press, 1964,
    71-101.

Benoit, Pierre. "Qumran and the New Testament," in Jerome
    Murphy-O'Connor, ed. *Paul and Qumran*. Chicago,
    Illinois: The Priory Press, 1968, 1-30.

Beyer, Hermann. "Blessing in Judaism at the Time of Jesus,"
    Theological Dictionary of the New Testament. 9 vols.
    G. Kittel and G. Bromiley, eds., G. Bromiley, trans.
    Grand Rapids, Michigan: William B. Eerdmans Publishing
    Company, 1965, 2, 759-765.

Bruce, F. F. "Jesus and the Gospels in the Light of the
    Scrolls," in Matthew Black, ed. *The Scrolls and
    Christianity*. London: The Talbot Press, 1969, 70-81.

Davies, W. D. "Gospel According to Matthew," in James
    Hastings, ed., Frederick Grant and H. H. Rowley, eds.,
    Revised Edition. *A Dictionary of the Bible*. New York:
    Charles Scribner's Sons, 1963, 630-633.

Delorme, J. "The Last Supper and the Pasch in the New
    Testament," in J. Delorme, P. Benoit, J. Dupont,
    M. E. Boismard, and D. Mollat. The Eucharist in the
    New Testament. E. M. Stewart, trans. Baltimore,
    Maryland: Helicon Press, 1964, 21-67.

Harrison, R. K. "The Rites and Customs of the Qumran Sect,"
    in Matthew Black, ed. The Scrolls and Christianity.
    London: The Talbot Press, 1969, 26-36.

Kuhn, Karl. "The Two Messiahs of Aaron and Israel," in
    Krister Stendahl, ed. The Scrolls and the New Testament.
    New York: Harper and Brothers, 1957, 54-64.

Kuhn, Karl. "The Lord's Supper and the Communal Meal at
    Qumran," in Krister Stendahl, ed. The Scrolls and the
    New Testament. New York: Harper and Brothers, 1957,
    65-93.

Mally, Edward. "The Gospel According to Mark," in R.
    Brown, J. Fitzmyer, and R. Murphy, eds., The Jerome
    Biblical Commentary. Englewood Cliffs, New Jersey:
    Prentice-Hall Inc., 1968, 21-61.

McKenzie, John L. "The Gospel According to Matthew," in
    R. Brown, J. Fitzmyer, and R. Murphy, eds. The Jerome
    Biblical Commentary. Englewood Cliffs, New Jersey:
    Prentice-Hall, Inc., 1968, Section 43, 62-114.

McNicol, J. "The Gospel According to Luke," in Francis
    Davidson, ed. The New Bible Commentary. Grand Rapids,
    Michigan: William B. Eerdmans Publishing Company,
    1965, 840-842.

Sparks, H. F. D. "Luke," in James Hastings, ed., Frederick
    Grant and H. H. Rowley, eds., Revised Edition. A
    Dictionary of the Bible. New York: Charles Scribner's
    Sons, 1963, 596-598.

Stanley, David and Brown, Raymond. "Aspects of New Testament
    Thought," in R. Brown, J. Fitzmyer, and R. Murphy, eds.
    The Jerome Biblical Commentary. Englewood Cliffs,
    New Jersey: Prentice-Hall, Inc., 1968, Section 78,
    768-799.

Stuhlmueller, Carroll. "The Gospel According to Luke," in R. Brown, J. Fitzmyer, and R. Murphy, eds. *The Jerome Biblical Commentary.* Englewood Cliffs, New Jersey: Prentice-Hall, Inc., 1968, Section 44, 115-164.

Swift, C. E. "Mark," in Francis Davidson, ed. *The New Bible Commentary.* Grand Rapids, Michigan: William B. Eerdmans Publishing Company, 1965, 804-806.

PERIODICALS

Box, G. H. "The Jewish Antecedents of the Eucharist," *Journal of Theological Studies*, 1902, III, 357-369.

Brown, Raymond E. "Second Thoughts on the Dead Sea Scrolls and the New Testament," *The Expository Times*, October, 1966, LXXVIII, 19-23.

Cameron, S. W. "The Intention of Jesus' Action at the Last Supper," *Modern Churchman*, March, 1959, 2, 150-157.

Cranfield, C. "Gospel of Mark," *The Interpreter's Dictionary of the Bible.* 4 vols. George A. Buttrick, ed. New York: Abingdon Press, 1962, 3, 267-269.

Cullmann, Oscar. "The Significance of the Qumran Texts for Research into the Beginnings of Christianity," *Journal of Biblical Literature,* 1955, LXXIV, 213-226.

Driver, Geoffrey. "Mythology of Qumran," *Jewish Quarterly Review,* April, 1958, LXI, 241-281.

Funk, Robert. "The Wilderness," *Journal of Biblical Literature,* 1959, 78, 205-214.

Groh, John E. "The Qumran Meal and the Last Supper," *Concordia Quarterly Monthly,* May, 1970, 41, 279-295.

Higgins, A. G. M. P. "A Few Thoughts on the Dead Sea Scrolls," *Modern Churchmen,* January, 1970, 13, 198-201.

Hjerl-Hanson, Borge. "Did Christ Know the Qumran Sect?"
    Revue de Qumran, July, 1958-July, 1959, I, 495-508.

Jeremias, Joachim. "The Theological Significance of the
    Dead Sea Scrolls," Concordia Theological Monthly,
    September, 1968, 39, 557-571.

Kilpatrick, G. D. "Living Issues in Biblical Scholarship,
    The Last Supper," The Expository Times, October, 1952,
    64:I, 4-8.

Mann, C. S. "The Scrolls, the Lord and the Primitive Church,"
    The Church Quarterly Review, October-December, 1958,
    159, 512-531.

Mowry, Lucretta. "The Dead Sea Scrolls and the Background for
    the Gospel of John," The Biblical Archaeologist,
    December, 1954, XVII, 78-97.

Priest, John F. "The Messiah and the Meal in IQSa," Journal
    of Biblical Literature, March, 1963, 82, 95-100.

Pryke, John E. "Beliefs and Practices of the Qumran
    Community," The Church Quarterly Review, July-September,
    1967, 168, 314-325.

Rowley, H. H. "The Qumran Sect and Christian Origins,"
    Bulletin of the John Ryland's Library, 1961-1962,
    XLIV, 141-145.

Stagg, Frank. "The Lord's Supper in the New Testament,"
    Review and Expositor, Winter, 1969, 66, 5-14.

Sutcliffe, Edmund F. "Sacred Meals at Qumran?" Heythrop
    Journal, 1960, I, 48-65.

Teicher, J. L. "Jesus Sayings in the Dead Sea Scrolls,"
    Journal of Jewish Studies, 1954, 6.

Van Der Ploeg, J. "The Meals of the Essenes," Journal of
    Semitic Studies, April, 1957, 2, 163-175.

Zeitlin, Solomon. "The Dead Sea Scrolls: A Travesty on Scholarship," <u>Jewish Quarterly Review</u>, 1956-1957, XLVII, 1-3, 6.

Zeitlin, Solomon. "The Hebrew Scrolls and the Status of Biblical Scholarship," <u>Jewish Quarterly Review</u>, 1951, 42, 133-192.

DATE DUE